Pass It On

Kaleidoscope

Statement of Purpose

Kaleidoscope is a series of adult educational resources developed for the ecumenical church by Lancaster Theological Seminary and the United Church Board for Homeland Ministries. Developed for adults who want serious study and dialog on contemporary issues of Christian faith and life, Kaleidoscope offers elective resources designed to provide new knowledge and new understanding for persons who seek personal growth and a deeper sense of social responsibility in their lives.

Kaleidoscope utilizes the expertise of professionals in various disciplines to develop study resources in both print and video. The series also provides tools to help persons develop skills in studying, reflecting, inquiring critically, and exploring avenues of appropriate Christian responses in life.

Kaleidoscope provides sound and tested resources in theology, biblical studies, ethics, and other related subjects that link personal growth and social responsibility to life situations in which adult Christian persons develop.

Pass It On

Telling and Hearing Stories from John

Gilbert L. Bartholomew

*Combined Leader's Guide and
Student Edition*

A Kaleidoscope Series Resource

United Church Press
Cleveland, Ohio

Kaleidoscope Series

United Church Press, Cleveland, Ohio 44115
© 1992 by United Church Press

Cover and book design by

Printed in the United States of America
The paper used in this publication is acid free and meets the minimum requirements of American National Standard for Information Sciences-Permanence of Paper for Printed Library Materials, ANSI Z39.48-1984

97 96 95 94 93 92   5 4 3 2 1

Bartholomew, Gilbert Leinbach.
        Pass it on : telling and hearing stories from John / Gilbert L. Bartholomew.
            p. cm.–(A Kaleidoscope series resource)
        Includes leader's guide.
        Includes bibliographical references.
        ISBN 0-8298-0886-8
        1. Bible stories, English–N.T. John. 2. Bible. N.T. John–Criticism, interpretation, etc. 3. Bible N.T. John–Reading. 4. Storytelling in Christian education. I. Title. II. Series.
    BS2615.5.B375 1992
    226.5'09505–dc20   92-30565
                                                                            CIP

*To my parents
Emma and Gilbert Bartholomew
who both tell and live the stories of Jesus*

*and to my wife Jane
who supports and encourages me
to pass the stories on*

Contents

Introduction to the Kaleidoscope Series

Through direct experience, our faculty at Lancaster Theological Seminary discovered that a continual demand exists for Christian theological reflection upon issues of current interest. To meet this demand, the Seminary for many years has offered courses for lay people. To offer the substance of these courses to the wider Christian public is the purpose of the Kaleidoscope Series.

Lancaster Seminary exists to proclaim the gospel of Jesus Christ for the sake of the church and the world. In addition to preparing men and women for the ordained Christian ministry, the Seminary seeks to be a center of theological reflection for clergy and laity. Continuing education and leadership development for all Christians focus our mission. The topics and educational style in the Kaleidoscope Series extend Lancaster Seminary's commitment: theological study reflective of Christians' interaction of the Bible, the world, the church, worship, and personal faith. We hope that this course will provide an opportunity for you to grow in self-understanding, in knowledge of other people and God's creation, and in the spirit of Christ.

We wish to thank the staff of the Division of Education and Publication of the United Church Board for Homeland Ministries for their support in this enterprise. The Rev. Dr. Ansley Coe Throckmorton, The Rev. Dr. Larry E. Kalp, and The Rev. Dr. Percel O. Alston provided encouragement and support for the project. In particular, we are grateful for the inspiration of Percel Alston, who was a trustee of Lancaster Seminary. His life-long interest in adult education makes it most appropriate that this series be dedicated to him. Two other staff members have guided the series through the writing and production stages: The Rev. Willard Wetzel, Project Coordinator for the Kaleidoscope Series, and The Rev. Nancy G. Wright, Editor for Kaleidoscope. As a publishing staff they have provided valuable experience and counsel. Finally, I wish to recognize the creative leadership of Jean Vieth, the Seminary Coordinator for the Series, who has been active for several years in this educational program at Lancaster.

Peter M. Schmiechen, President
Lancaster Theological Seminary

How to Use the Kaleidoscope Series

The Kaleidoscope book is the basic resource for all students in the Kaleidoscope Series. In each Kaleidoscope book there is a Leader's Guide bound into the back of the book. The leader will need to study both the text and the Leader's Guide to prepare to lead study sessions of the Kaleidoscope Series resources. The accompanying video is a very helpful tool for the class using this book as a study resource.

Other KALEIDOSCOPE resources are

- *BREAD FOR THE BANQUET: Experiencing Life in the Spirit*, by Elaine M. Ward
- *THE GIFT AND THE PROMISE: Becoming What We Are in Christ*, by Peter Schmiechen
- *GOD, WHERE ARE YOU? Suffering and Faith*, by Richard F. Vieth
- *NOBODY'S CHILD: A Generation Caught in the Middle*, by Paul E. Irion
- *STRETCH OUT YOUR HAND: Exploring Healing Prayer*, by Tilda Norberg and Robert D. Webber
- *THUNDER ON THE RIGHT: Understanding Conservative Christianity*, by Elizabeth C. Nordbeck
- *JOURNEY THROUGH THE PSALMS: A Path to Wholeness*, by Denise Dombrowski Hopkins
- *BECOMING PEOPLE OF THE WAY: Intentional Christianity*, by Francis Ringer
- *INTIMACY: The Quest for Life Connections*, by James W. Hanna

Preface

In the 1950s I attended grade school in Philadelphia. Each morning we students took turns reading from the Bible. The rule stated ten verses a day. This meant that sometimes the reader would stop dead at the end of the tenth verse, whether or not the story was at an end!

Most of us experience Bible reading that way. Little bites of ten verses or even less. Often a part of a story or a few verses of a psalm. Sometimes only one brief, albeit significant, verse!

Modern translations of the Bible into everyday language invite us to read beyond the ten verse limit, to become involved in whole stories, letters, visions, and poems. The text is laid out in paragraphs instead of single verses; headings often summarize the content. These simple devices encourage us to start at a sensible beginning point and stop only when we get to the end.

Oral reading may also help make larger portions of the Bible far more digestible. Indeed, a good oral reader or a storyteller can make the Bible so alive that listeners will sit for a whole series of Bible stories—even an entire Gospel!

The Gospel of John is one sustained narrative of the ministry, death, and resurrection of Jesus. Individual segments, often interlocked, are frequently rounded out by extended conversations or reflections to bring out the full meaning of the incident.

In this resource book I have focused on six of John's stories. They are quite long, as stories from the Gospels go. In each of them action plays a prominent role, conversation is lively and fast moving, and the event or encounter comes to a resolution. These six stories connect with other parts of John's Gospel and can be properly understood only within the context of the Evangelist's entire narrative. To appreciate these stories' larger significance, we must begin by reading them aloud in their entirety, and in a way that brings out all the dramatic and lifelike qualities they possess.

I hope that as you read and study these six stories from the Gospel of John, you will appreciate how wonderful they are to read and to hear from beginning to end. The characters are vivid; the events and conversations, the struggles and the transformations are true to life.

I have another purpose in writing this book. As we listen to stories from the Bible, we often hear echoes of our own experiences. The echoes may be clear or very faint. But we sense that the Bible stories are not only about events in the dim and ancient past; they are also about our lives today.

We need to try to remember the particular incidents in our lives that make a Bible story feel more or less familiar. Remembering, we may give thanks that our lives are in harmony with the will of God for us, or we may repent and seek to be transformed.

As a stimulus to your memory, I have included in each chapter a few stories from my own life and the lives of people I know. Sometimes the link between my contemporary story and the biblical story is slight, but through it my life begins to approach the Gospel of John. And my story may suggest a more fitting connection for you.

Personal experiences happen in community with others and the impetus for writing this book is no exception. I first learned to love the Bible through the lives and teachings of my mother and father, early Sunday School teachers, junior choir directors, and a host of other Christians who were members of the congregations of my childhood and adolescence. More recently, I was enticed into the fascinating world of modern biblical study by my professors Paul J. Achtemeier, J. Louis Martyn, and Rudolf Schnackenburg. My enjoyment of biblical narratives as lively and life-transforming oral events is a gift of my colleague Tom Boomershine. I have been privileged to share that gift with students, pastors, parishioners, and members of the Network of Biblical Storytellers. Special thanks go to Pam Moffat for reading much of the manuscript and for her challenging honesty, and to Ruth Kershner for sharing her skill in proofreading.

The context for sharing and reflecting upon Bible stories has been my work as a teacher of New Testament at Lancaster Seminary and as a pastor to United Church of Christ congregations in the Cumberland, Perry, and Schuylkill counties of Pennsylvania. Through the greater part of my life, my wife Jane has offered a partnership full of joy, encouragement, and appreciation within which to pursue this challenging, sometimes frustrating, but in the end always rewarding vocation.

Pass It On

Telling and Hearing Stories from John

Chapter One

Prejudice and Oneness in Christ

The Woman of Samaria
John 4:1–42 (Author's Translation)

For an explanation of the words and phrases that are underscored and in bold type, see page 11.

Scene 1. The Setting

[1] So when Jesus found out that the Pharisees had heard that Jesus was making and baptizing more disciples than John [2] —and yet Jesus himself was not baptizing, but his disciples were—[3] he left Judea and went away again to Galilee. [4] Now he had to go through Samaria.

[5] So he comes to a city of Samaria called Sychar, near the field which Jacob gave to Joseph his son. [6] Now that was the location of Jacob's well.

So Jesus, weary from the journey, was sitting like that at the well. The hour was about noon. [7] Along comes a woman of Samaria to draw water.

Scene 2. Jesus and the Woman

Jesus says to her, "Give me a **drink**." [8] (His disciples, you see, had gone off into the city to buy provisions.) [9] So the Samaritan woman says to him, "How can you, who are a Jew, ask for a **drink** from me, who am a Samaritan woman?! Jews don't have anything to do with Samaritans!"

[10] Jesus answered and said to her, "If you knew the gift of God and who it is who is saying to you, 'Give me a **drink**,' you would have asked him, and he would have given you **living water**." [11] The woman says to him, "Sir, you don't have a bucket, and the well is

1

deep. So where do you have the **living water** from? [12] Are you perhaps greater than our father Jacob who gave us the well and he himself drank from it, and his sons, and his flocks?"

[13] Jesus answered and said to her, "All who drink this water will be **thirsty** again. [14] But those who drink the water I shall give them shall not be **thirsty** ever, but the water I shall give them will become in them a well of water bubbling up to eternal life." [15] The woman says to him, "Sir, give me this water, so I won't be **thirsty** or have to come here to draw!"

[16] He says to her, "Go call your **husband** and come back." [17] The woman answered him and said, "I don't have a **husband** ." Jesus says to her, "Well said, 'I don't have a **husband**.' [18] You see, you have had five **husbands**, and now the one you have is not your **husband**! This you have said truthfully."

[19] The woman says to him, "Sir, I perceive that you are a prophet. [20] Our ancestors worshiped on this **mountain**, yet you people say that in Jerusalem is the place where one must worship." [21] Jesus says to her, "Believe me, woman, the hour is coming when neither on this **mountain** nor in Jerusalem will you people worship the Father.

[22] You worship what you do not know; we worship what we know, for salvation is from the Jews. [23] But the hour is coming, indeed now is, when the true worshipers will worship the Father in **spirit** and in truth. For it is such people the Father is seeking as those who worship him. [24] God is **spirit**, and those who worship him must worship in **spirit** and truth."

[25] The woman says to him, "I know that the Messiah is coming, who is called Christ. When he comes, he will make everything known to us." [26] Jesus says to her, "I am he, who speak with you."

Scene 3. The Disciples

[27] And just then his disciples arrived. And they marveled that he was speaking with a woman. No one, however, said, "What do you want?" or "Why are you talking with her?"

Scene 4. The Woman

[28] So the woman left her water jar. And she went off into the city and she says to the people, [29] "Come see a man who told me

everything I've done! <u>Is this man the Christ maybe?</u>" [30] They went out of the city and started off in his direction.

Scene 5. *The Disciples and Jesus*

[31] In the meantime, the disciples were begging him, "Rabbi, eat!" [32] But he said to them, "I have food to eat that you don't know anything about."

[33] So the disciples began to say to one another, "Has someone perhaps brought him something to eat?" [34] Jesus says to them, "My food is to do the will of the one who sent me, and to accomplish his work.

[35] "Aren't you accustomed to saying, 'Four months yet, then the harvest comes'? Look, I tell you. Lift up your eyes and see the fields, that they are ripe for the harvest already! [36] The reaper is receiving his wages, and gathering fruit for eternal life, so that at the same time the sower may rejoice along with the reaper.

[37] "In this, you see, the saying is true, 'One sows and another reaps.' [38] I sent you to reap that for which you have done no labor. Others have labored, and you have entered into their labor."

Scene 6. *The Samaritans and Jesus*

[39] Now many of the Samaritans of that city believed in him because of the word of the woman, who bore witness, "He told me everything I've done." [40] So when the Samaritans came to him, then started begging him to stay with them. And he stayed there for two days.

Scene 7. *The Samaritans and the Woman*

[41] And many more believed because of his word, [42] and they were saying to the woman, "No longer because of your word do we believe. For we ourselves have heard, and we know that this man is truly <u>the savior of the world</u>."

How Bible Characters Feel

Several years ago, I was having lunch with two seminarians, Linda and Jim. We were experimenting with different ways of reading aloud the story of Jesus' conversation with the Samaritan woman beside the well. Despite the difficulty of doing this while eating peanut butter sandwiches, we made some exciting discoveries.

For instance, how would you say the words of the woman in verse 9: "How can you, who are a Jew, ask for a drink from me, who am a Samaritan woman?" Jim tried it. In his version the woman sounded respectfully surprised. Linda read. The woman's words were filled with sneering sarcasm.

How did the Evangelist first present this Samaritan woman to his listeners? It occurred to us that his last words in the verse, "Jews don't have anything to do with Samaritans," could explain hostility as well as surprise on the woman's part. Linda's sneering sarcasm seemed to be a real possibility. Our interest was piqued. We began to dig into our commentaries and Bible dictionaries for more information. From them we learned that in ancient times the relationship between Jews and Samaritans went up and down like a yo-yo.[1] And during the period in which Jesus lived and John composed his Gospel, the feelings were spinning at the very end of the string. The Jewish historian Flavius Josephus, born shortly after Jesus' crucifixion and a contemporary of John the Evangelist, tells of an incident that took place in A.D. 6-9 [2] and illustrates this conflict:

> During the administration of Judaea by Coponius . . . an event occurred which I shall now describe. When the Festival of Unleavened Bread, which we call Passover, was going on, the priests were accustomed to throw open the gates of the temple after midnight. This time, when the gates were first opened, some Samaritans, who had secretly entered Jerusalem, began to scatter human bones in the porticoes and throughout the temple. [3]

Commenting on this incident, Joachim Jeremias, an outstanding modern scholar, says: "This was obviously an act of revenge for something about which Josephus is characteristically silent. This appalling defilement of the Temple, which probably interrupted the Passover feast, added fresh fuel to the old fires of hatred." [4]

In light of this conflict, Linda, Jim, and I asked ourselves: "If I had been a woman living in Samaria back in the first century A.D. and a Jew asked me for a drink, how would I have felt about him and his request?" If others think they are too good to associate with me until they need something, what is my reflex response? Am I "mincing and coy with a certain light grace," [5] as one commentator says of this woman? Or am I shocked and contemptuous?

This experiment with various ways of reading the words of a character in a biblical story, ways based on historical clues about how that character may have felt, helped us crack open a hard shell of pious niceness that robs the characters of the rich variety of feelings, including those harsh or even nasty feelings that make up so much of our daily experience.

Understanding the climate of hostility within which the conversation between Jesus and the woman of Samaria takes place, Linda, Jim, and I turned once more to the beginning of the story. We wondered, would other parts take on new life as we played with new ways of reading the words? Would we hear the stories afresh if we looked into Bible study resources to see what might lie behind the stories?

Bible Reading in the Church

Have you ever tried to interpret a Bible story by experimenting with different ways of reading the words of the characters? Have you ever asked yourself, If I had been in the shoes of that person in the story, how would I have felt?

What a difference these questions can make! As we fill the printed words with the emotions we ourselves would have felt had we been in their place, the people of the Bible suddenly step out of the book, and like Pinocchio, turn into "a real boy" with a conscience and the ability to grow a very long nose when telling a lie. When we make Bible characters live they become our companions along life's sometimes smooth but often rocky roads.

Our style of reading the Bible aloud in church is often encased in traditions we seldom question. Indeed, we are often not even aware of a style of reading until suddenly offered an alternative. One of the styles that prevails (at least in many white churches in North America and parts of Europe) is that of reading scripture with as little emotional vividness and variety of expression as possible. If we feel an intensity about what we are reading and manifest it in our interpretation, we risk censure for being over dramatic. Sadly our fears bar us from playing with different ways of reading the words, from asking, "How would I have felt if I had been there?"

Yet when the early Christians read the Bible aloud, in all probability they read in a way we would call dramatic. Amos Wilder says that "when we picture to ourselves the early Christian narrators we should make full allowance for animated and expressive narration. In ancient times even when one read to oneself from a book, one always read aloud. Oral speech was also less inhibited than today." [6]

An animated reading of a Bible story has a remarkable effect on both the reader and the listener. A dispassionate reading, by the same token, can turn the text into a dry puzzle. We need an emotionally vivid and varied reading if we are to turn the story into an event in which we find ourselves participants. Such a reading draws us out of the stands onto the playing field. It absorbs us in suspense-filled and shocking action. We feel sympathy with some characters and antipathy towards others. And we recognize ourselves. In this way the biblical story begins to resonate with our own story.

As we experiment with various ways of speaking the words of a biblical story, it is important to try out many possibilities. At some point, however, we move beyond the question "How would I have felt if I had been that character?" to "How would I have felt *if I had lived in Palestine or Samaria two thousand years ago?*"

With this in mind, let us return to the beginning of the story of Jesus' conversation with the Samaritan woman at the well and approach it from the twofold perspective: (1) the characters speaking as we ourselves would speak in their situation, and (2) the same protagonists talking as men and women of their own times, some two thousand years ago. Perhaps the woman, Jesus, and his disciples will all step off the page fully alive and become the companions of our daily experience. Perhaps they will even take us by the hand and lead us back into their own world to share in their experience of long ago. Either way, we may find our lives illumined by the light of the gospel, or even transformed by its power.

The Story's Setting

The story of the Samaritan woman is artfully fashioned in seven scenes. Each is marked by a change of character or place. In the translation above, I have labeled these scenes to be immediately recognizable to a reader.

The first scene begins with the voice of the narrator, John the Evangelist. He leads us forward from a previous act in his larger drama of the life of Jesus to this new one. The Pharisees know that Jesus is making more disciples than John the Baptist. For some undisclosed reason, this leads Jesus to leave Judea for Galilee. And then we hear the lead-in to the story of Jesus and the Samaritans: "Now he had to go through Samaria."

This simple statement is a loaded one. Samaria is enemy territory for Jews like Jesus and his disciples. They go through it when they have to in order to get from one Jewish area to another in a reasonable length of time. When the Evangelist read this story to his first-century listeners, he surely made a pregnant pause at this point to allow the implications of this statement to sink in. If he were making a television production of his story today, he would no doubt sound the ominous Dragnet theme, "Dun d'dun dun. Dun d'dun dun. Du-u-un." The air hangs heavy with the threat of a storm.

The ancient fight between Jews and Samaritans is not our fight, however. How can we enter into this story with a true appreciation of how the characters must have felt? Think of a time in your life when you had to travel through a place that filled you with anxiety.

For two years I attended Union Theological Seminary in New York City. For two years Jane and I lived on the edge of Harlem (a section of the city notorious for its crime and violence). I neither had nor took the opportunity to get to know people who lived there. And I avoided everything in that section of the city but a Chinese restaurant, a supermarket, and a laundromat, all of which were on its very edge.

When it came time to move out of the city, I scanned the Yellow Pages and found the closest place to rent a truck. There was a Hertz office just five blocks up Broadway from the school. So a few days before moving day, that is where I went to reserve a van.

On moving day I learned to my horror that the truck was not at the Hertz office just five blocks up the street. It was all the way over on the other side of the city. And to get there I was going to have to take a bus straight across Harlem. And I was going to have to carry $100 along with me—in cash! As I walked to the bus stop, for me the air hung heavy with foreboding.

The Evangelist moves on with his story. Jesus comes to the Samaritan city of Sychar. Jesus and his disciples have been walking in the sun, and it is now the middle of the day. Jesus sits down wearily beside Jacob's well while his disciples go into the city to buy food. "Along comes a woman of Samaria to draw water." Dun d'dun dun. The air hangs even heavier. It is one thing to travel through territory that fills us with anxiety. It is another for the specter of danger to materialize into a concrete, threatening person.

What will happen in this confrontation between Jesus and this woman? That is the question that governs this entire story. We have the stage setting for the series of encounters that will flow out of it. But before the action develops, there is another suspense-filled pause.

Jesus' Conversation with the Woman

The silence of a pause is broken by a thunder clap that jolts us right out of our seats—at least if we had lived in the Evangelist's own time and place it would have jolted us out of our seats. Jesus says to the woman, "Give me a drink." To someone who knows how Jews and Samaritans felt about each other, this is an utterly shocking request.

A Jewish man did not talk with a woman in public. The Mishnah, a collection of rabbinic teachings compiled in about A.D. 200, records this admonition of Jose ben Johanan of Jerusalem, a scribe who lived about 150 B.C.: "Talk not much with woman-kind." To this the Mishnah adds, "They said this of a man's own wife: how much more of his fellow's wife!" [7] The closest we can come to this prohibition is in the fundamentalist Muslim world today. We in the West are likely to be as shocked by this wide-spread and age-old prohibition of public contact between a man and a woman as ancient listeners were at Jesus' violation of it.

To make matters worse, this woman with whom Jesus began this conversation is a *Samaritan!* She is a member of a group of people who shared with the Jews a mutual hatred. Ritual purity was a fundamental concern in Jewish religious practice, and if anyone was likely to be impure, it would be a Samaritan woman. According to Leviticus 15:19–30, one form of impurity was a woman's menstrual flow. Again, the Mishnah records a rule from the last decades before the destruction of the Temple in A.D. 70: "The daughters of the Samaritans are [deemed unclean as] menstruants from their cradle."[8]

It would have been bad enough, then, if Jesus had merely begun to speak with this woman. But what he actually said to her in opening the conversation would surely have been the most profoundly shocking thing imaginable: "Give me a drink." Natural though it may seem to ask for a drink while resting beside a well in the middle of the day after a long walk, a Jew would simply not have wanted to drink from anything a Samaritan had touched. This is why the woman in John's story responds to his request with utter astonishment. She knows that "Jews don't have anything to do with Samaritans" (v. 9b); or, in the words of the Good News Bible, "Jews will not use the same dishes that Samaritans use."

How did Jesus' listeners probably respond to his request? Did you ever feel revulsion at the prospect of sharing something as personal as a drinking vessel with someone you felt was "unclean"?

My friend Larry was in the army in Japan. He told me that once at the altar rail he took communion from a common cup. Larry is white. The man to drink before him was black. Larry said he knew it was wrong, but he just couldn't bring himself to drink.

Such a story is not pleasant to tell. But how often an incident like this is repeated! Jesus sought to minister to and transform the most perverted of human relationships. Unless we bring them out to where they can collide head-on with Jesus' story, how can they have any chance of being "totalled" and replaced by a new story?

We all agreed—Linda, Jim, and I—that the woman's response to Jesus expresses astonishment that this Jew should make such a request. No doubt her astonishment was also bitter and her words to Jesus full of derision. How do we feel when a person treats us rotten except when in need of our help?

Earlier I mentioned that there are two translations of the woman's shocked response to Jesus: "Jews don't have anything to do with Samaritans," and "Jews will not use the same dishes that Samaritans use." All translations with which I am familiar present this sentence as a comment by John, an explanation to his audience of something they might not understand. The translators indicate this by closing the quotation at the end of the woman's question and enclosing this line in parentheses. But another alternative emerged while Linda, Jim, and I played with the woman's words.

We discovered that the last sentence in verse 9 could be part of the woman's derisive response to Jesus. He asks her for a drink, and she hurls in his face the care his people always take not to contaminate themselves through contact with Samaritans. Nothing prohibits us from reading the sentence in this way. The earliest Greek manuscripts contain virtually no punctuation, in fact, they do not even separate the words! The quotation marks and parentheses of modern translations are devices developed over the centuries to make reading easier. So there is no reason that we cannot choose a translation in which the woman herself explains angrily and defiantly her shock by throwing in Jesus' face the deep antipathy Jews had for her people, the Samaritans.

I have spent much time discussing the opening verses of this story because these verses are often not read at all, and rarely with the plausible oral interpretation Jim and Linda and I discovered. Worship leaders gravitate to the theological gems in this story, like "the water that I shall give them will become in them a well of water bubbling up to everlasting life," and "God is spirit, and those who worship him must worship in spirit and truth." The worship leaders either omit or make short shrift of the setting within which those gems are presented.

The Evangelist, however, has carefully chosen this setting for showing off the theological jewels. And it is hard to imagine a setting that could better exhibit the beauty of the gems he has bequeathed to us. The setting is a relationship of painful hostility between two closely related peoples. If this point is lost sight of, we bypass and may misunderstand the intent of the author of the Gospel.

Let us continue with the story to see how it moves beyond the tragic circumstances and experience in which it begins. The first major movement of the story is scene 2, the conversation between Jesus and the woman (vv. 7b-28). It develops artfully in seven parts. The first six are each dominated by a different word or phrase: *drink, living water, thirsty, husband, mountain, spirit.* This list makes it clear that the first three parts are closely joined. They focus on water and move from Jesus' own request for a drink to his climactic offer of water that is "bubbling up to eternal life." In verse 16 the conversation takes a decided turn. The theme of water is left behind and Jesus and the woman focus on the question of true worship. Weaving in and out of the whole series of seven parts and sewing them together is the question, Who is this Jew who asks this Samaritan woman for a drink? (These six key words and phrases and the words related to the identity of Jesus are highlighted in my translation so that you may locate them easily.)

There are many important things we could attend to in this conversation. Let's look at three. First, the phrase *living water* would not have struck an ancient Jew who spoke Greek as immediately symbolic. *Living water* was the phrase for the flowing water of a well or spring in contrast to the stagnant water collected in a cistern. It was precisely the kind of water that a person with a bucket could draw from Jacob's well! In Genesis 26:19, for example, the ancient Greek translation speaks of a "well of living water." In the course of Jesus' conversation with the Samaritan woman, not only the water but also the descriptive word *living* turn out to be symbolic. There is precedent for the symbolic use of this phrase in the Greek translation of Jeremiah, which was widely read by Greek-speaking Jews of the Evangelist's day: "For my people have done two things and evil things: they have forsaken me, a spring of living water, and they have dug out for themselves broken cisterns, which will not be able to hold water [Jer. 2:13]."

It is also important to understand what Jesus means when he declares, first, that "neither on this mountain nor in Jerusalem will you people worship the Father," and then that "true worshipers will worship the Father in spirit and in truth." He is not contrasting external forms of worship with worship that goes on within the human spirit. Instead, he is pointing to the impermanence of an "earthly" rather than a "heavenly" way of regarding religious institutions. The temples on Mt. Gerezim ("this mountain") and in Jerusalem, on the one hand, are contrasted to the freedom of God's Spirit to "blow where it wills [John 3:8]" on the other. The temple on Mt. Gerezim already lay in ruins, and the Temple in Jerusalem would follow it before too many years had passed. People with an earthly point of view make a commitment to such institutions the test of true worship and condemn the worship of others who don't pass this test. Jesus knows God respects no such test. Indeed, to set aside a special place for worship can be a great aid to worship. But God's Spirit, rather than the place of worship, is the test of true worship. God, who is worshiped and who is the source of worship, determines whether one truly worships, not the place. It is also very clear in John that God gives the Spirit to those who believe in Jesus.

A third matter of significance is the way Jesus speaks here about worshiping "the Father." In our day we can no longer take for granted the language the Bible uses for God. Nor dare we assume that we have a correct understanding of it. We need to engage constantly in "biblical criticism." This theological term does not refer to an effort to criticize the Bible, but an effort to subject our own current understanding of the Bible to the critical question "Is this what the ancient author of the biblical text really meant?" Biblical criticism requires us to surrender our favorite ideas if someone can demonstrate more authentic interpretations. In understanding Jesus' use of the word "Father" for God in the Gospel, we must remember that for John the only way to know God is through Jesus (1:18). As Son, Jesus does only what he sees the Father doing (5:19). What sort of father does Jesus reveal God to be by his words and actions? [9]

Important as it is to know the meaning of the phrase *living water* and the meaning of *spiritual worship* and worship of *the Father*, it is equally essential to understand what is happening to the Samaritan woman in the course of the conversation and the effect it may have on the reader or listener. Clearly the woman is beginning to discover who this Jew is who asked her for a drink. The seeds of her faith are still to burst into flower; they will bear fruit later in the story. Here, however, Jesus plants those seeds through a series of shocking, strange, and astounding words. He begins with the initial request for water, progresses through his promise to give her living water that will satisfy her thirst forever, goes on to his prophetic insight that she has had five husbands and is now living with a man to whom she is not married, and ends with his declaration—astonishing on the lips of a Jew—that the hour is coming when even Jerusalem will not be the place of true, spiritual worship of the Father.

In the course of hearing Jesus' words, the woman changes. She first makes fun of him for claiming to be greater than Jacob the patriarch. Then she declares he must be some kind of prophet. Finally, she turns her mind to the coming Messiah.

Her words to Jesus show a gradual change in her attitude. She begins with derisive hostility. But her rhetorical question about

how he compares to Jacob, in verse 12, is more mocking than
hostile. It amounts to "Just who do you think you are!" In verse
15 her tone is more, "Don't I wish you could do what you say!" In
verse 19 she is perhaps embarrassed at Jesus' prophet-like knowledge of her life. And in verse 25 she has become pensive in the
light of what he has been saying to her.

Both the change in the woman's words and the change in her
attitude toward Jesus blossom into full faith in later scenes of the
story. Her own next words are an excited witness to Jesus' miraculous knowledge of her life, followed by an equally excited, though
tentative, question "Just maybe, could this be the Christ [v. 29]?"
The answer is given by the people of the city who first rush off to
see Jesus for themselves, then beg him to stay with them, and in
the end exclaim, "This man is truly the savior of the world [v. 41]!"

In reading or listening to this story, even today we can be caught
up in the excitement of new faith aborning, new faith made all the
sweeter when it comes into being in the midst of hatred and
bitterness between Jews and Samaritans. That is the setting in
which John has bequeathed to us the deeply moving statements
about Jesus' nature and that which he gives us towards which we so
quickly gravitate.

One could hope also that our own faith today can come alive in
settings where there is hostility and divisiveness. Here is an
experience of mine that connects with this story. It is not an exact
parallel, because it is not about new faith in Jesus, but it tells about
my discovery of the faith an old enemy already had in Jesus.

In the early 1950s I lived in Philadelphia where I attended a local
public school. The kids on our block who went to parochial school at the
local Catholic church would turn around and spit on the backs of us
Protestants as we passed each other in the alley on our way to school. It
was a religious and ethnic split similar to the ancient split between Jews
and Samaritans. But over the years, beginning not too long after the
Second Vatican Council, I had many memorable experiences in which I
came to know the deep faith Roman Catholics have in Jesus. I give one
example. Through my father-in-law, I became acquainted with a priest,
Msgr. Sowers, who in turn introduced me to Sr. Kathleen Kirk. She
was interested in learning Greek, and I had written an introduction to
New Testament Greek. For several years I visited her monastery near

Towson, Maryland. At first we mainly studied Greek. But as time went on we ate together, made music together, she on the organ and I on my trumpet, learned stories from the Bible together, and participated in the prayer and worship life of her community together. As I came to know her faith in Jesus, Jesus truly became for me the Savior of the world and the well of living water that bubbles up to eternal life. And my faith sparkles the more brightly because it is set against the background of a childhood conflict into which Jesus has brought reconciliation!

Enter the Disciples

We return now to John's story. The joy of seeing and experiencing the transformation of the Samaritan woman's hostility towards Jesus into faith in him is not all there is to the story, thrilling though that may be. Like Luke's parable of the prodigal son, John's story has two parts. In the first part of Luke's parable the lost is found. In the second part the older brother, who remained faithfully at home, witnesses the music and dancing occasioned by the lost son's return. Will the "elder" disciples in John's story look kindly on the hospitality Jesus is extending towards this woman whose past makes her so offensive and undeserving? Their unspoken thoughts at seeing him talking with her show that Jesus will have as much work to do converting them to accepting her as he had converting her to accepting him.

Like the father in Luke's parable, Jesus will plead with his disciples to welcome the woman that he has with such lack of propriety run out to meet. And like Luke, John will end his story without telling us how Jesus' Jewish disciples finally responded to the Samaritans converted by the woman or how they responded to Jesus' presence among their former enemies.

Let us follow the second half of John's story as it unfolds. The disciples return to Jesus before the woman has really shown any signs of faith in Jesus. The things he had been saying to her gradually turned her mind toward the Messiah, for whom the Samaritans, like the Jews, longed. And Jesus declares that he is the very one for whom the Samaritans are looking.

But then, in a master stroke of what seems like bad timing, the disciples return and interrupt the conversation! But perhaps the timing is not all that bad. Jesus has done what he could. The rest is up to the woman.

The return of Jesus' disciples (v. 27) puts us back at square one in the relationship between the Jews and the Samaritans. When Jesus addressed the woman, she burst out with the venomous question, why was *Jesus* wanting anything from *her?* Now, when the disciples see Jesus speaking with her, their minds are filled with a similar and presumably equally hostile question, what does Jesus want from *her?* or why is he talking with *her?* The disciples restrain themselves from uttering their question aloud. But both they and the woman wonder why Jesus is addressing her. And the root of the objection of both is the enmity between Jews and Samaritans.

The disciples' objection is in terms of the fact that Jesus is talking in public with a *woman*. As listeners we can hardly have forgotten the fact that she is also a *Samaritan* woman. Jesus' behavior challenges both the Jewish rule regarding the way he as a man should behave in public toward a woman and the rule about the way he as a Jew should act toward a Samaritan. In the ensuing conversation Jesus pleads for the disciples to reach out to the Samaritans who are coming out of the city. Jesus thus seeks to break down the dividing wall of hostility both between Jews and Samaritans and between men and women.

Before Jesus tackles the attitude of his disciples toward the woman, John narrates another brief incident crucial to how Jesus will respond to the disciples' unspoken objection. The arrival of this bunch of scowling men is an effective conversation stopper. So the woman, without finishing her task of fetching water or encumbering herself with her water jar, hurries back into the city. There she rehearses in front of others the event that has captured her attention, and she tentatively tries out on them her own question: "Could this be the Christ, just maybe?" The people of the city hurry off to see Jesus. They are longing for the Christ too. They are ripe for the plucking. And it is to this fact that Jesus then directs his disciples' attention.

Jesus' conversation with his disciples in verses 31 through 38 is the counterpart of his conversation with the woman in verses 7b through 26. She hotly pointed out that "Jews don't have anything to do with Samaritans." They in disgust think to themselves, "What are you talking with her for?" Jesus tries to convert her hostility toward him because he is a Jew to belief in him despite the fact he is a Jew. Then he tries to convert his disciples to acceptance of her and her fellow townspeople, despite the fact she is a woman and they are all Samaritans. Jesus began the conversation with the woman with a request, "Give me a drink." His disciples begin their conversation with him with a corresponding request, "Rabbi, eat!" Jesus' next words to the woman are that he has water for which she should have asked him. His next words to the disciples are that he has food that they don't know anything about. The woman responds to Jesus' offer of water with the question of where is he going to get that water without a bucket. The disciples respond to Jesus' declaration that he has food with the question of how can he have food unless perhaps someone brought him some. Jesus tells the woman that the water he shall give her will become a well of water bubbling up to eternal life. He tells his disciples that the harvest that is even now being gathered in is a harvest of fruit for eternal life.

Jesus appeals to his disciples with two major, related images. The first is that of food: the second, that of the harvest. Jesus' food is to do the will of the one who sent him. His disciples don't yet know anything about that food, just as the woman does not yet really know anything about the water Jesus is offering her. Jesus suggests that his conversation with the woman satisfied his physical hunger as satisfactorily as if he had eaten bread.

One evening, arriving home from a day of teaching in Lancaster and visiting several people at the Reading hospital, I learned that an elderly couple needed to see me right away. I was dead tired and hungry. With a sigh I hopped right back in the car and went to see them. Their niece and some close friends from the church were there trying to deal with a crisis. As we sat and talked, we began to iron out the situation. And I began to feel refreshed by the progress we made and the good company. It was as effective as a snack and a good night's sleep!

The second image in Jesus' appeal to his disciples is that of the harvest. He declares to them that doing the will of God is food for which they must still develop a taste and in which they must learn to find satisfaction. Then he directs their attention to the Samaritan people of the city who have responded to the woman's witness to Jesus. Jesus has sowed the seed of faith among the Samaritans in his conversation with the woman. And the harvest is instantaneous! Is the woman the reaper who is gathering among her fellow townspeople fruit for eternal life? In any case, here come Samaritans who are ripe for being gathered into the community of believers, which up until this time has consisted only of Jesus' disciples, who are Jews. The disciples did not plant the seed of faith among the Samaritans—and they probably would not have wanted to do so. They'd rather harvest more Jews like themselves. But here is the ripe grain: the Samaritans who are right in front of their eyes! Now harvest it, Jesus commands them!

We were on a youth retreat. And a few of the boys were desperately trying to get their friends to join them in a volleyball game. But all to no avail. The other boys were involved in something else and didn't want to play. Meanwhile one of the less attractive girls was hanging around the boys, punctuating their pleas to the other boys with, "I'll play, I'll play volleyball with you!"

Jesus' appeal to the disciples to "gather in" the Samaritans will come as no surprise to those of us who have been listening closely to John's story from the beginning. Jesus has prepared us for it in his conversation with the woman. But throughout that conversation it is clear that Jesus himself is a Jew. As a Jew he is the object of the woman's venomous attack. He makes no effort to deny his Jewishness. He even asserts that "salvation is from the Jews." Though the Samaritans later recognize him as "Savior of the world," he comes as a person of a particular cultural and religious heritage. The cultural and religious particularity of the means of revelation in the Bible continues to be an important element of both Judaism and Christianity. And it is offensive to many people. Why should a definitive revelation of God be connected with a particular people or person? Such thinking is intolerable in a pluralistic society!

Notice, however, that even though Jesus is clearly Jewish, he disregards two matters of central importance to his people's religious practice: ritual cleanness and worship in Jerusalem. He places worship of the God of his people on a different footing, namely, commitment to a person, the Messiah, who gives the water of life, the Spirit of truth, the source of true worship of the Father.

We must not miss the implications of this for the disciples as harvesters. Harvesting does not mean bringing the Samaritans into a community in which they will replace Samaritan religious practices with Jewish ones. Harvesting means bringing the Samaritans into a community of persons who believe that the Jew Jesus is the true revelation of God and giver of the Spirit out of which flows a life of worship, a life that satisfies completely and forever.

What will be the earthly particulars of this community's worship? The silence of the Gospel of John on this matter, together with the emphasis on belief in Jesus, suggests that the particulars of worship will be culturally varied or brand new. They will not be completely devoid of outward form in favor of a worship totally internal—something impossible to achieve unless we are relieved of our bodies. The particulars of worship will, however, cease to be a barrier between believers.

As a modern Christian, perhaps you will say, "Of course becoming a Christian does not mean becoming a Jew." But the story also says to us that being a Christian does not necessarily involve specific religious practices, ones that particular groups of modern Christians may hold to be essential to Christianity!

A number of years ago I was serving a church in a small town in Pennsylvania. And a new family moved to town from New Jersey. The family consisted of a mother, her three children, and her parents. All the members of the family became quite active in the church. They were talented and very willing to use their talents to serve the church. But it quickly became clear that their church in New Jersey had not always done things the same way we in Pennsylvania were doing them. Furthermore, many older members were offended that this new family wanted to change some things instead of remolding themselves to fit in.

Our custom on Maundy Thursday was to have an upper room celebration of communion around tables in our church basement. Before the service began, the children came to me very excited. Could they take communion? Even though they had not been confirmed, they had been allowed to take communion in their church in New Jersey. Perhaps I should have said a firm "No, that is not the way we do things here." But instead, I told them to make their own decision. As we sat eating the bread, the woman across from me sat craning her neck to see the children at the other end of the row of tables. She looked horrified as she watched them also eating the bread.

When the Spirit of God brings us together with other Christians who come from different religious and ethnic traditions, should we not expect that we will all be transformed? John's story strongly suggests we will, not only when we unite with other Christians, but even when we bring new believers into the church! When in word and deed we appeal to non-Christian people to put their faith in Jesus and they say yes for the first time in their lives, do we set out to remold them in our image, what we think it means to be a Christian? Or do we open ourselves to the transforming power of God's Spirit working through them?

The Savior of the World

In the final scenes of John's story, the Samaritans put their faith in Jesus, first of all because of the woman's testimony to his miraculous knowledge about her life. But after he has remained in their city for two days, they testify to her that on hearing him they have learned firsthand that he is the Savior, not just of Jews, but of Samaritans also, indeed of the whole world.

The story has come to its climax: faith in Jesus, not secondhand faith based on the testimony of another, but firsthand faith rooted in an encounter of one's own. But the faith of the Samaritans is more than simply faith in Jesus; it is faith in Jesus *as Savior of the world*. The Samaritans accept as *their* Savior a person *of another ethnic group!* And for Jesus' Jewish disciples and any of John's listeners who are Jewish, that means a Savior through whom their own ethnic particularities are relativized—not denigrated, but put in their proper place in relation to the particularities of another ethnic group.

What then of my faith? Of your faith? Is it secondhand faith or firsthand faith? Is it faith that excludes, that cuts us off from other persons, even other believers whose culture and experience is different from our own? Or is it faith that includes, that unites us to, all kinds of people, many of whom are radically different from us?

I, like many of you who will be reading this book, was brought up believing in Jesus. As I reflect on my faith, I realize that it has always been a mixture of secondhand and firsthand faith. As a child I learned the song

Jesus loves the little children,
All the children of the world.
Red and yellow, black and white,

They are precious in his sight.
Jesus loves the little children of the world.

And I believed in Jesus as Savior of the world. But it became firsthand faith for me when missionaries of other races and nationalities stayed as guests in our home, and my parents showed the same love for them as they had always shown towards me.

Some Christians would say that I am still talking about secondhand faith. For some, firsthand faith is an emotional experience of Jesus' presence that leaves a person with no doubt whatever that Jesus is real. But firsthand faith can come in other forms as well. When I experience love from a person of another race and recognize it as the love Jesus showed in stories in the Bible, I experience firsthand what the stories are talking about. When I listen to a story of Jesus and become caught up in it and feel moved and inspired by what Jesus says to people and how he treats them, that is a firsthand experience of the events of the story. It begins to reshape and nurture my daily life. When I hear the story of Jesus in Samaria and remember my anxiety as I rode the bus through Harlem, Jesus' words to the woman and to his disciples in the story address me firsthand. And when I enjoy music with Sr. Kathleen, I know firsthand the love of Jesus that unites us in our differences and makes the lives of us all far richer.

Coming to a firsthand belief in Jesus does not necessarily involve a change from having heard about him but not believing in him at all, to being totally convinced of his living presence, perhaps through some emotional experience. It may also mean an attraction to him through what others say about him that then begins an ongoing process of reflecting, interpreting, and reshaping my own daily experience.

Chapter Two

The Gift and Cost of Sight
The Man Born Blind
John 9:1–41 (Author's Translation)

Scene 1. Jesus' Healing of the Man Born Blind

¹ And while he was going along, he saw a man who had been blind from birth. ² And his disciples asked him, "Rabbi, who sinned, this man or his parents, that he was born blind?" ³ Jesus answered, "Neither this man sinned, nor his parents, but that the works of God might be revealed in him.

⁴ "We must work the works of the one who sent me while it is day. Night is coming, when no one can work. ⁵ As long as I am in the world, I am the light of the world."

⁶ After he said this, he spat on the ground and made mud from the saliva and rubbed the mud on his eyes. ⁷ And he said to him, "Go, wash in the pool of Siloam" (which means "sent"). So he went, and washed, and came back seeing!

Scene 2. The Man and the Neighbors

⁸ So the neighbors and those who had previously been accustomed to seeing him as a beggar began to say, "Isn't this man the one who used to sit and beg?!" ⁹ Some said, "This is the one!" Others said, "No, but he looks like him." He said, "I am the one!"

¹⁰ So they said to him, "How then were your eyes opened?" ¹¹ He replied, "The man called Jesus made mud and rubbed it on my eyes and said to me, 'Go to Siloam and wash.' So I went and washed and received my sight."

¹² And they said to him, "Where is he?" He said, "I don't know."

Scene 3. The Man and the Pharisees

¹³ They bring him to the Pharisees, this formerly blind man.
¹⁴ Now it was a Sabbath Day when Jesus made the mud and
opened his eyes.

¹⁵ So again they questioned him—the Pharisees this time—how he
received his sight. He said to them, "He put mud on my eyes, and
I washed, and I see."

¹⁶ So some of the Pharisees said, "This man is not from God, for
he does not keep the Sabbath." But others said, "How can a man
who is a sinner do such signs?" And there was a division between
them.

¹⁷ So they say to the blind man again, "What do you say about
him, since he opened your eyes?" He said, "He is a prophet."

Scene 4. The Pharisees and the Man's Parents

¹⁸ So the Jews did not believe that he had been blind and
received his sight, until they sent for the parents of the one who
had received his sight. ¹⁹ And they asked them, "Is this your son,
who you say was born blind? How then does he now see?"

²⁰ So his parents answered, "We know that this is our son and
that he was born blind. ²¹ But how he now sees we don't know, or
who opened his eyes we don't know. Ask him. He's an adult; he
will speak for himself."

²² His parents said these things because they were afraid of the
Jewish authorities. For the Jewish authorities had already agreed
that if anyone should declare his belief that he was the Christ, he
would be excommunicated from the synagogue. ²³ This is the
reason that his parents said, "He's an adult, ask him."

Scene 5. The Man and the Pharisees

²⁴ So they sent a second time for the man who had been blind.
And they said to him, "Give glory to God. We know that this man
is a sinner."

²⁵ So he responded, "I don't know whether he is a sinner. I
know one thing, that although I was blind, I now see."

²⁶ So they asked him, "What did he do to you? How did he
open your eyes?"

²⁷ He answered, "I already told you, and you didn't listen. Why do you want to hear again? Surely you don't want to become his disciples, too!"

²⁸ And they heaped abuse on him and said, "You are that man's disciple, but we are disciples of Moses. ²⁹ We know that God spoke to Moses, but we don't know where this man is from!"

³⁰ The man responded, "This is incredible that you don't know where he is from, yet he opened my eyes. ³¹ We know that God does not listen to sinners. But if a person is devout and does the will of God, God listens to that person. ³² No one has ever heard of someone opening the eyes of a man born blind! ³³ If this man were not from God, he would not be able to do anything."

³⁴ They replied, "You were born in complete and total sin, and you presume to teach us!" And they threw him out!

Scene 6. The Man and Jesus

³⁵ Jesus heard that they had thrown him out. And he found him and asked him, "Do you believe in the Son of man?" ³⁶ He answered, "Tell me who he is, sir, that I may believe in him?" ³⁷ Jesus said to him, "You have seen him, and the very person who is speaking to you is the one." ³⁸ And he said, "I believe, Lord!" And he prostrated himself before him.

Scene 7. The Pharisees and Jesus

³⁹ Jesus said, "For judgment I have come into the world, so that those who have no sight may see, and so those who see may become blind." ⁴⁰ Some of the Pharisees who were within earshot heard this and said to him, "Surely you don't mean that even we are blind!" ⁴¹ Jesus said to them, "If you were blind, you would have no sin. But now you say, 'We see!' Your sin remains!"

That the Works of God Might Be Revealed

During my senior year in college, I served as student assistant pastor at a United Presbyterian church about a half hour north of Pittsburgh, Pennsylvania. The first Sunday there, I was greeted cheerily after the morning worship service by David. David had Down's syndrome.

What a family David was born into! Mother, father, older sister and brother, all rallying around him, sharing the heartache, but also experiencing the wonder of David's uninhibited love.

Did David's parents ever wonder, "What did we do wrong that our child was born with Down's syndrome?" How many parents of handicapped children must be nagged by that question, even though their good sense tells them that God does not send sickness as a punishment for sin!

David's handicap was, as a popular book puts it, a bad thing that happened to good people. David's family was good, some of the most dedicated and loving Christians I have ever met.

I don't know whether David's parents struggled with the question "Why did this happen to us?" They probably did. What I do know for certain is that David's handicap had become an occasion for the works of God to be revealed in the life of their family. It caused them much pain. They missed him when he was away at a special school for long stretches of time. But their faith that God was at work in their lives and their God-given strength to endure their suffering brought forth a bumper crop of love.

I think of David's family every time I hear or read the story of Jesus' healing of the blind man in John 9. The disciples asked him the question that for millennia has plagued people who long to believe that the world is ruled by justice rather than by chance. Jesus rejected the "sin theory" of suffering, at least in this case if not in all cases. (See Mark 2:1–12 where his response to a person's paralysis is first of all forgiveness.) He saw the blind man's suffering as an opportunity for the works of God to be revealed.

If this raises the even more difficult question "How can a loving God permit unjust suffering?" then at least Jesus has left God in the dock in place of innocent sufferers. In this instance Jesus relieves the man of his suffering as well as of the shame of guilt. He also challenges us to move beyond the question of the guilt, both of the man and of God, to see his healing as the power of God made manifest in a person stigmatized as a sinner.

The Shock Waves of Change

John 9 begins with Jesus center stage, healing a lifelong sufferer of physical and spiritual distress. But in a short time the spotlight swings away from Jesus, and the story opens up into a seven-scene drama about the consequences of this life-changing event for the man's ties to his community. For the next four scenes the focus of attention is the man, not Jesus.

A miracle, we are made to realize, is not always an unmixed blessing. A dramatic change in the life of one person can be very upsetting to those around. There is often a cost if a person is to gain. The negative reactions of the formerly blind man's community are the subject of the following scenes.

The entire drama is an occasion for us to recall and reflect upon deep changes in our own lives and the often negative response of family, neighbors, and the leaders of our church and community. These changes and resulting conflicts are more often moral, relational, and cultural than explicitly religious. Often, however, they grow out of religious commitment. The Bible story may also shed new light on the ways we have handled sudden or gradual change in persons whose lives impinge upon our own.

Our friend Jill suffered for years from a disease that sapped her strength and was gradually causing her to go blind. During that time she relied on traditional medicine, but to no avail. Then she met a physical therapist named Russell. He not only helped her to recover but almost perfectly restored her sight. How did he do this? He taught her how to relax and get rid of the tension she stored up in her body. He laid warm hands on her. He placed a crystal in her hand, which would become very warm. He himself would sleep with a crystal on his own body at the place she was experiencing distress. Like the formerly blind man in John's story, Jill assures others that she was once drained of physical strength and almost blind. And she enthusiastically tells others what Russell did to heal her. Her story gets mixed responses. Some people welcome the testimony to an alternative medical approach to healing. Others are skeptical, even hostile.

* * *

Tom [1] and I were in graduate school together, working for a doctorate in New Testament. While serving as pastor of a city church, he began telling and hearing the stories in the Bible the way I am inviting you to tell and hear them in this book, and he rediscovered their transforming power. In the world of biblical scholarship, this was a brand new approach to the biblical narratives. It raised new questions and called for new methods of study. Tom devoted his dissertation to demonstrating how his new approach releases from the stories a power they did not seem to have when approached in traditional ways. It took some years for Tom to get across to me what he had discovered. Many in the community of biblical scholarship had little patience for his approach.

* * *

Ella married Ralph four years ago. The beginning of their relationship was not peaceful. During the few years immediately before their marriage, most of their energy went into helping Ralph to deal with very serious problems. Not so long ago Ella came to talk with me. She has begun to discover some new dimensions of herself. A group at church has helped her explore and develop these new dimensions. Ella longs to share the changes in herself with Ralph. She needs him at least to listen. He doesn't want to hear it. He does not want her to change.

These three stories are just a few examples of the deep changes that come about in us and of their repercussions. To be alive means to change. The changes may be physical, intellectual, or spiritual. Rarely can we keep them to ourselves. They often have profound implications for our life with others. They may have an impact, not only upon a few close associates, but upon the entire fabric of the culture within which we live.

Our cultural traditions tend to resist changes and put them to the test. Rightly so. For not every challenge to tradition is healthy or accurately interpreted by the challenger. Challenges to traditions and habitual ways of perceiving them may be the work of God, but they may also be the fruit of human sinfulness. However, the custodians of tradition need to test proposed changes in a spirit of humility and openness. They need to assume unseen imperfections and outright falsehoods in the structure and even in the foundations of the tradition. Tradition can at best bear witness to the truth; it cannot definitively and forever describe it. (See Jesus' words to that effect in John 5:39–47.)

Often, however, those who are charged with the responsibility to uphold tradition regard it as the final and exclusive statement of truth. If they derive their power from the tradition's authority, they often employ coercive methods to maintain that tradition, instead of letting it stand or fall by virtue of its own strengths or weaknesses.

Recall your own stories of change and growth and how others around you received them. Perhaps you took an unpopular position on a national or social issue, such as war and peace or the way to deal with drugs and drug users. Maybe you felt compelled to give up a harmful habit of speech or behavior, like racial slurs or alcohol abuse, that helped bind you to family and friends. Recall also such changes in those around you—family members, friends, neighbors—that had an impact on you. How are your stories like that of the blind man? How are they different? Does John's story bring you new sight? Is that new sight a work of God in your life? Is it God's way of offering you new life? Will receiving that gift also carry with it some sort of cost?

The Man and the Neighbors

Having related in John 9:1-7 the healing of the blind man, the Evangelist moves to his main concern. In seven scenes he plays out the results of being healed by Jesus, as the man encounters the people with whom he has to live. Their responses are clear.

The first thing that happens is that the neighbors and others see the man no longer doing what he had always done (vv. 8-12). It is that simple. After being healed he did not go around telling people what happened, the way the Samaritan woman ran off to tell the people of Sychar how Jesus had miraculously "read" to her the story of her life. He merely began to live in a way required by the change Jesus had brought about in his life: Now able to see, he could, at the very least, no longer sit and beg.

And the change does not go unnoticed. "Isn't this man the one who used to sit and beg?" they ask. Some say, "This is the one!" Others say—and you can just hear the ridicule in their voices—"No, but he looks like him." At this point the man must speak. Either he must deny what Jesus has done for him, or he must bear witness to it. The formerly blind man responds joyfully, "I am the one!" But at this point in John's Gospel, to bear witness to a relationship with Jesus is to court trouble.

Whenever I hear this brief exchange between the man and his neighbors, I think of Jill. She enthusiastically tells the story of being healed by Russell. But all my life I have assumed that

scientific medicine is exclusively adequate for sickness. And so my
reflex is to respond, "No, it just looks as though Russell's uncon-
ventional methods healed you."

Once the formerly blind man testifies to being healed by Jesus,
the cross-examination begins. "How then were your eyes opened?"
people want to know, and the man describes what Jesus did.
"Where is he?" they ask, presumably anxious to meet Jesus and
question him firsthand; but here the formerly blind man cannot
oblige. And so the neighbors and others take him to the authorities who are charged with responsibility for evaluating such claims.

How typical all this is of responses to life-changing experiences
and insights today. Since Jill claimed that Russell had healed her, I
wanted to know exactly what he did, and I wanted to meet him so I
could question him myself. Ultimately, I wanted to subject Jill's
healing to the scrutiny of the reigning healing tradition in our
culture.

The Pharisees and Others

Now in the Gospel story the cross-examination of the formerly
blind man intensifies (vv. 13–17). Now his claim must stand the
test, not of ordinary people like the neighbors, but of authorities in
tradition. He is commanded to repeat the story of his healing. He
does so, and at first these authorities accept his healing as fact. But
then a new element is introduced.

What is at issue changes immediately from whether and how the
man received his sight to the acceptability of the healer. Some of
the authorities object to the healing because Jesus showed disregard
for long-standing rules of the community regarding the Sabbath.
Others are so impressed by what Jesus did that they are ready to
overlook his disregard for the rules. So we see that at first the
authorities cannot agree on what to make of Jesus and his act of
healing. In other words, the experts differ, so they force the cured
man to move beyond bearing witness to his healing to making a
judgment about the one who healed him! Receiving physical sight
now becomes an occasion for new spiritual sight. It is not just a
question of who Jesus is. What the man thinks of Jesus connects
to his view of the importance of physical healing in contrast to
maintaining the traditional rules regarding the Sabbath.

Similarly, Jill's healing has raised questions for her that go far beyond concern for the means by which one might be healed. She has been led by that experience to a view of the nature of the world very different from the view governing modern medical science. However, even within the scientific community today, some people are raising questions about the adequacy of traditional scientific theory. Today's experts are split in their evaluation of other life-changing, culture-altering experiences as well. Many women and men, for example, have discovered serious drawbacks in the pervasive and millennia-old male orientation of our culture and church. Their discoveries have led them to new patterns of acting and speaking. Other people hotly debate the validity of the new insights.

Division among the authorities now disappears from view; from this point (John 9:18) they speak with one voice. They call in the man's parents to verify the claim that the man was indeed blind (vv. 18-23). And the father and mother testify that he is indeed their son, that he was born blind, and that clearly he has received his sight. But they refuse to have anything to do with the authorities' central concern: who did it and how? They direct attention back to their son himself. Perhaps they do so because they simply don't know the answer to the authorities' questions. But they also don't want to get further involved. To do so is to wade into dangerous waters.

The majority of the Jewish leaders have already concluded that Jesus is unacceptable to them in light of his challenges to the tradition. And they are intent on barring him from gaining any more disciples by excluding him and his disciples from the community. This threat of exclusion hangs over the heads of the healed man's parents and ominously suggests what will happen to the formerly blind man if he perseveres in his positive evaluation of Jesus.

This experience is repeated in today's controversies. Our polarized society readily excludes those who disagree. When I am among people who make their position on war and peace, human sexuality, or New Age impulses in our culture very clear, I tend to hold back from expressing an opposing view for fear of condemnation. Exclusion may well be the price of an alternative way of seeing things. I have even held back from trying to gain a hearing for the experiences and insights of some of my friends. When I do this, I am doing exactly what the formerly blind man's parents do: I am abandoning them to their own defense.

Finally, in verses 24–34 the authorities deliver an ultimatum to the formerly blind man. They open this new examination of him with the exhortation, "Give glory to God," the same exhortation given by Joshua in Joshua 7:19 before he condemned Achan and his family and everything that Achan owned to destruction. The authorities then reiterate the earlier verdict of the majority that Jesus is a sinner. They are no longer open, if they ever were, to the possibility that Jesus' miraculous healing in any way commends him.

But the man will not back down from asserting the authority of his experience over that of the tradition. And his conviction leads him to a view of Jesus diametrically opposed to that of the authorities: How can a person who has healed him from lifelong blindness be anything but an agent of God?

The healed blind man is now as committed to the goodness of Jesus as the authorities are committed to Jesus' sinfulness (vv. 30–33). They have forced him to choose between Jesus and themselves. And what follows is an argument that only serves to reinforce the conclusion each party has already reached about Jesus. It heats up the negative feelings between the man and the authorities until their relationship explodes.

In the course of this scene, the authorities repeat an earlier question, the man loses his patience and becomes sarcastic, the authorities in turn become abusive, the man insults them. Finally the authorities have had enough. They turn from the discussion about Jesus to attacking the man himself. He, like Jesus, is a sinner, obviously born in sin by virtue of his blindness. The view of such a one is for them obviously of no account!

And so they cut the man off from the community. They close the doors of the synagogue in which he was brought up and at home, closing off from him all its celebrations and customs. They prohibit any further contact with his family and friends.

This kind of argument and its results are all too familiar in present-day life. Within families a spouse or a child experiences an

event that entails a new view of life. When she or he expresses a
desire to pursue that new life, the response is solid resistance. And
soon both sides are out to win, not to seek to understand and
appreciate a different point of view. Tempers flare, sarcastic and
abusive language increases, positions and people are condemned,
questions ignored instead of answered.

As a result of such arguments the person is often shunned.
Within a family the dissenters may continue to live in the same
house but lead separate lives; or a husband and wife may divorce;
or a child who feels ignored may be driven from home. A religious
community may avoid contact with distrusted people and give them
the cold shoulder.

Jesus and Others

The story of the Samaritan woman's conversation with Jesus
dramatized the way belief in Jesus leads people who are alienated
from each other into new community with one another. This story
of the healing of the man born blind plays out the price of being
led into a new community of relationships to Jesus Christ. Belief in
Jesus may first cause alienation from those with whom we have
spent our entire lives.

The blind man has to pay a high price for Jesus' gift of sight—
not of physical sight, but of spiritual sight. Because he sees Jesus'
work of healing as evidence that Jesus must be from God and
cannot be a sinner, because he sticks to that insight in the face of
the most powerful challenge, he suffers one of the severest penal-
ties, exile from the only community and culture he has ever known.

But Jesus does not abandon him. Having heard what the
community authorities did to the man, Jesus now reenters the
picture and offers the man a relationship with himself (vv. 35-38).
The experience is often repeated today.

*A woman in our church finds help and fulfillment by giving her time
and abilities to various church programs. Her husband is on the road a
good bit of the time but resents the fact that she doesn't sit home all day
waiting for him. And so the members of our congregation go out of their
way to express appreciation for what she does and for the difficulties of
her relationship with her husband.*

* * *

A young man's father won't talk to him because he decided to go to college instead of joining the family business. I make a special effort to keep contact with the young man, to be an ear as he struggles with his isolation from his father and seeks to maintain his enthusiasm for his chosen career.

In the last scene of the story (vv. 39–41), Jesus confronts the community leaders with the significance of what they have done to the blind man he has healed. He announces the double purpose in his work: "So that those who have no sight may see, and so those who see may become blind." He addresses his words to no one in particular. He is simply articulating a truth about why he has come.

Some of the authorities are close enough to hear him. They understand him to imply that they are the ones who are blind. And Jesus assures them of the correctness of their deduction. These words of Jesus are actually only the first few sentences of a long dialogue with the authorities, which continues through John 10:21 and ends with a reference to his healing of the blind man. That dialogue contains Jesus' well-known words about the good shepherd. (It is too long to consider here, but note that it is a continuation of Jesus' response to the authorities begun in 9:41 and that in it Jesus picks up on an important Old Testament image for the leaders of Israel. See Jeremiah 23:1–6; Ezekiel 34.) Jesus contrasts the authorities' destructive actions towards people like the formerly blind man to his own care for them. John 9:39–41 also exhibits a familiar pattern of argument.

Sometimes after I have been arguing with someone and getting nowhere, I'll turn away and, perhaps while I am walking out the door, I make a general remark like, "Some people are just too blind to see what's in front of them." I don't address it directly to my opponents, but I mean it as a judgment against them. And someone hears me say it and comes running after me, shouting, "Hey, what do you mean by that?!"

John 9: An Anti-Jewish Story?

Many people today find a story like that in John 9 to be offensive. They regard it as an expression of the fourth evangelist's "anti-Judaism." The term refers to Jews cast as villains while Christians are cast as heros. It ends with a condemnation of the leaders of the Jews as blind.

To come to this conclusion, however, is to forget the role of "Pharisees" and "Jews" within the community—that of authorities charged with the preservation of the tradition and granted the power to do so. The stories of contemporary experience related in this chapter should make it clear that the community leaders in John's story exemplify the kind of behavior to which all persons in a position of power are prone. And it is not only the custodians of tradition who use their power to coerce. When the champions of new insights gain power, they often use it in the same way. Witness, for example, how abominably Christians treated Jews after Christianity became the official religion of the Roman Empire.

It is important to understand, however, that the historical controversy echoed in this story was not a controversy between two religions, Judaism and Christianity. It was a controversy *within Judaism* over the question of whether or not Jesus was the long-awaited Messiah. A relatively small group of Jews came to believe that he was. But their faith presented a challenge to the traditional interpretation of Torah and to the authority of the leaders of the Jewish community who were charged to uphold it. Faith in Jesus as Messiah led believers to open the community of Israel to all peoples, solely on the basis of a shared belief in Jesus, without any need to adopt the Jewish religious practices required by the Torah, such as Sabbath observance. This liberalism ran directly counter to the Pharisees' focus on observing precisely those Torah commands that distinguished Jews from other peoples and thus helped maintain their identity. How could these two approaches to what it means to be a Jew coexist?

We experience a similar problem within the Christian church today. We do not argue about *whether* the Messiah is to be *found in Jesus*. But we do argue about *where* Jesus the Messiah *is to be found*. We believe that Jesus Christ is risen from the dead and present in the community as a living, powerful Spirit. But where is

the Spirit of Jesus at work? Among Pro-Life or Pro-Choice advo-
cates? Among those who promote the use of inclusive language in
worship or those who argue vigorously against it? Among the
champions of Gay Rights or those who press for the traditional
view of biblical morality? Among those who want their church to
move to a community they are "better equipped to serve" or among
those who contend that the church must serve the people on its
doorstep?

These are some conflicts in which modern Christians believe
Jesus Christ is living out his life in the Christian community today.
But the issue is not whether the older way of seeing things will
forcibly eliminate the new, but how Christians with differing views
are treating each other. The Christian community is often as
polarized and mutually hostile and alienated as was the Jewish
community in John's story.

Conclusion

Life means growth and growth means change. Changes in the
life of one person have repercussions in the lives of those around.
Traditions need to be honored; they help keep new insights
responsible. And within the Christian church our traditions help
us to struggle with the question, "Is this life-changing event or
insight in my life the Spirit of the living God at work in me?" But
no tradition, not even a Christian tradition, may be idolized as the
final expression of truth, as valid for all times and places, and as
containing no inadequacy, weakness, or evil.

When a person experiences a life-changing event, the fruit of that
experience often has a price tag. The first cost is that of bearing
witness to what has happened. The second is that of defending it
under cross-examination. A third cost may be abandonment by
friends and family; a fourth, the suffering of condemnation. A
final cost may be exclusion from the community that has played an
important and precious role in one's life. If that happens, we may
hope that there will be a new community to welcome us.

Being forced to leave behind our old family, friends, and
neighbors in order to grow is tragic. How tragic that others are
sometimes so threatened by new experiences and insights that they

cannot tolerate them! How tragic that people are then forced to choose between their discoveries about life and their home community.

But such conflicts have a long history within the human race. And this dramatic narrative in John 9 contains all the dynamics of the way such a tragic conflict gets played out in people's lives. When we hear the story it reminds us of times when we too had to choose or when we forced others to choose. It should also alert us to the playing out of such tragic events in the future.

We for our part can hope that as we grow and change, our families, friends, and communities will be willing to maintain their relationship with us and we with them. We can strive to disagree in a spirit of love, to respect, understand, and appreciate, when we cannot agree. And we can labor to be more hospitable to others who are different. We can seek to follow the example of "a Pharisee in the council named Gamaliel, a teacher of the law" in Acts 5:34–39. When others wanted to kill the apostles for disobeying an order to cease and desist from preaching in Jesus' name, he said:

> Fellow Israelites, consider carefully what you propose to do to these men. For some time ago Theudas rose up, claiming to be somebody, and a number of men, about four hundred, joined him; but he was killed, and all who followed him were dispersed and disappeared. After him Judas the Galilean rose up at the time of the census and got people to follow him; he also perished, and all who followed him were scattered. So in the present case, I tell you, keep away from these men and let them alone; because if this plan or this undertaking is of human origin, it will fail; but if it is of God, you will not be able to overthrow them—in that case you may even be found fighting against God!

Chapter Three

Disappointment and Fulfillment

Mary and Martha
John 11:1-54

Scene 1. Lazarus and His Sisters in Bethany; Jesus Across the Jordan River

[1] Now a certain man was ill, Lazarus of Bethany, the village of Mary and her sister Martha. [2] Mary was the one who anointed the Lord with perfume and wiped his feet with her hair; her brother Lazarus was ill.

[3] So the sisters sent a message to Jesus, "Lord, the one you love is ill!" [4] But when Jesus heard it, he said, "This illness does not lead to death; rather it is for God's glory, so that the Son of God may be glorified through it."

[5] Now Jesus loved Martha and her sister and Lazarus. [6] So when he heard that Lazarus was ill, he stayed in the place where he was for two days!

Scene 2. Jesus and His Disciples Still Across the Jordan River

[7] Then after this he said to the disciples, "Let us go to Judea again." [8] The disciples said to him, "Rabbi, the Jews were just now trying to stone you, and are you going there again?"

[9] Jesus answered, "Are there not twelve hours of daylight? Those who walk during the day do not stumble, because they see the light of this world. [10] But those who walk at night stumble, because the light is not in them."

[11] After saying this, he told them, "Our friend Lazarus has fallen asleep, but I am going there to awaken him." [12] The disciples said to

37

him, "Lord, if he has fallen asleep, he will be all right." [13] Jesus, however, had been speaking about his death, but they thought that he was referring merely to sleep.

[14] Then Jesus told them plainly, "Lazarus is dead. [15] For your sake I am glad I was not there, so that you may believe. But let us go to him." [16] Thomas, who was called the Twin, said to his fellow disciples, "Let's us also go, that we may die with him."

Scene 3. Jesus and Martha Outside Bethany

[17] When Jesus arrived, he found that Lazarus had already been in the tomb four days. [18] Now Bethany was near Jerusalem, about two miles away, [19] and many of the Jews had come to Martha and Mary to console them about their brother.

[20] When Martha heard that Jesus was coming, she went and met him. But Mary stayed at home.

[21] Martha said to Jesus, "Lord, if you had been here, my brother would not have died. [22] But even now I know that God will give you whatever you ask of him."

[23] Jesus said to her, "Your brother will rise again." [24] Martha said to him, "I know that he will rise again—in the resurrection on the last day!"

[25] Jesus said to her, "I am the resurrection and the life. Those who believe in me, even though they die, will live, [26] and everyone who lives and believes in me will never die. Do you believe this?"

[27] She said to him, "Yes, Lord; I believe that you are the Messiah, the Son of God, the one coming into the world."

Scene 4. Jesus, Mary, and Mourners Outside Bethany

[28] When she had said this, she went back and called her sister Mary, and told her privately, "The Teacher is here and is calling for you." [29] And when she heard it, she got up quickly and went to him. [30] Now Jesus had not yet come to the village, but was still at the place where Martha had met him.

[31] The Jews who were with her in the house, consoling her, saw Mary get up quickly and go out. They followed her because they thought that she was going to the tomb to weep there.

[32] When Mary came where Jesus was and saw him, she knelt at his feet and said to him, "Lord, if you had been here, my brother would not have died."

[33] When Jesus saw her weeping, and the Jews who came with her also weeping, he became angry in spirit and shaken. [34] He said, "Where have you laid him?" They said to him, "Lord, come and see." [35] Jesus began to weep.

[36] So the Jews said, "See how he loved him!" [37] But some of them said, "Could not he who opened the eyes of the blind man have kept this man from dying?"

Scene 5. Jesus, Martha, Mary, and the Mourners at the Tomb

[38] Then Jesus, again inwardly angry, came to the tomb. It was a cave, and a stone was lying against it.

[39] Jesus said, "Take away the stone." Martha, the sister of the dead man, said to him, "Lord, already there is a stench because he has been dead four days."

[40] Jesus said to her, "Did I not tell you that if you believed, you would see the glory of God?" [41] So they took away the stone.

And Jesus looked upward and said, "Father, I thank you for having heard me. [42] I knew that you always hear me, but I have said this for the sake of the crowd standing here, so that they may believe that you sent me."

[43] When he had said this, he cried with a loud voice, "Lazarus, come out!" [44] The dead man came out, his hands and feet bound with strips of cloth, and his face was wrapped in a cloth. Jesus said to them, "Unbind him, and let him go."

Scene 6. The Chief Priests and Pharisees in the Temple

[45] Many of the Jews therefore, who had come with Mary and had seen what Jesus did, believed in him. [46] But some of them went to the Pharisees and told them what he had done.

[47] So the chief priests and the Pharisees called a meeting of the council, and said, "What are we to do? This man is performing many signs. [48] If we let him go on like this, everyone will believe in him, and the Romans will come and destroy both our holy place and our nation."

[49] But one of them, Caiaphas, who was high priest that year, said to them, "You know nothing at all! [50] You do not understand that it is better for you to have one man die for the people than to have the whole nation destroyed."

51 He did not say this on his own, but being high priest that year he prophesied that Jesus was about to die for the nation, 52 and not for the nation only, but to gather into one the dispersed children of God. 53 So from that day on they planned how to put him to death.

Scene 7. Jesus and the Disciples Beyond Judean Territory

54 Jesus therefore no longer walked about openly among the Jews, but went from there to a town called Ephraim in the region near the wilderness; and he remained there with the disciples.

Quoted Out of Context

A procession of automobiles drove slowly through the open gate, then on up the hill to the place where the green canopy had been temporarily erected. When everyone had gathered together under its shelter, the pastor began, "I am the resurrection and the life. Those who believe in me, even though they die, will live, and everyone who lives and believes in me will never die."

A familiar experience to you? Familiar words? Do you know where those words come from? When you hear them, does a whole scene come into your mind's eye: Martha and Jesus talking together on a dusty road just outside the village of Bethany, Martha with grief and distress written all over her face, Jesus pleading for her trust?

What is the shortest sentence in the Bible? "Jesus wept." Of course! But where in the Bible do we find it? And does it bring to mind Mary and Jesus on a dusty road just outside the village of Bethany, Mary on her knees at Jesus' feet, a group of mourners gathered around them, and everyone together weeping and wailing?

The story of the raising of Lazarus is a moving story. Yet how often is it shared in its entirety with a group of people? Many Christians are familiar with the words, "I am the resurrection and the life," and they know that "Jesus wept" is the shortest sentence in the Bible. But those words do not usually bring to mind the events that lead up to the moment that Jesus calls Lazarus forth from the tomb.

John's Story as My Story

It was in the middle of the story at the point of the encounter between Martha and Jesus, that I began to realize that my story and the events of Lazarus's story merge. How often as a pastor I have stood at a graveside and read Jesus' words "I am the resurrection and the life." And how often I have heard Jesus' next question and have wondered about my own response and that of those there at the grave with me: "Do you believe this?"

This oft-repeated experience started me on my way to hearing the whole of this story as my story. I have yet to lose to death anyone as close to me as my own brother, but I have been at the side of many people who have. I have shared their urgent prayers to God to come and save one God also surely loves, and I have watched as God delayed and the loved one died. I have heard many versions of Martha and Mary's anguished reproach, "Lord, if you had been here, my brother would not have died." I have joined in Martha-like resistance to the reality of death and pleaded with God to do something even when it was too late. I have wept with the loved ones when, like Mary, they resigned themselves to the fact that there was nothing more to be done.

Urgent Summons—Delayed Response

The story in John 11 opens by introducing us to a family we have not met up to this point in the Fourth Gospel. The only other place they appear in the New Testament is Luke 10:38-42. Luke makes no mention of Lazarus, but his portrayal of the contrasting personalities of Mary and Martha is very much like John's. (This is important to note for later.)

In John these sisters and their brother are very special to Jesus. The Evangelist first indicates their special relationship by "recalling" an incident he has not yet narrated, Mary's act of anointing Jesus' feet with oil and wiping them with her hair (12:1-8). John seems to assume that his readers or listeners already know about that event. By reminding them of it, he starts his story with a vivid picture of the warmth and intimacy between Jesus and this family. In the next several verses, John emphasizes the special quality of their relationship by speaking twice of Jesus' love for them (vv. 3, 5).

These close, good friends of Jesus are in the midst of a crisis. Lazarus is ill. So the sisters send a message to Jesus, "Lord, the one you love is ill!" Urgency bursts from the simplicity of the message. It is terse. It contains no explicit request. It merely describes the sisters' situation in a way that appeals to Jesus' own interest in it: The one who is ill is one Jesus himself loves! Jesus will surely act!

But what do the sisters expect Jesus to do? The answer is obvious to anyone who knows the Gospels. Jesus is a healer. In the Gospel of John itself, he has a reputation for healing (6:2), and the Evangelist has narrated three of his healings dramatically and in detail (the official's son (4:46-54), the lame man (5:1-13), and the blind man (9:1-7). On these other occasions Jesus healed people with whom he had no previous relationship. How eagerly he will surely respond now that he is being called upon to heal a man he loves!

Jesus does respond to the urgent summons. But how? First, with a word of reassurance: "This illness does not lead to death." Then with a deed: "He stayed for two days in the place where he was."

What a shocking way for Jesus to behave! Why does he act that way? After assuring us that Lazarus' illness is not unto death, he does nothing to prevent death from being the result. If he loves Martha and her sister and Lazarus, why does he not rush right off? Is it because he knows that Lazarus' illness is not as serious as the sisters think? Is it because he knows there is no cause for alarm?

The answer to our questions is not long in coming. The Evangelist continues: "Then after this he said to the disciples, 'Let us go into Judea again'." Judea is where Bethany is located. After a two-day delay Jesus decides it is time to respond to Mary and Martha's summons. His reason? "Our beloved friend Lazarus has fallen asleep." There has been a change in Lazarus' condition. When the sisters sent their message, the one he loved was "ill". Now after Jesus' two-day delay, his beloved friend has "fallen asleep."

But why go now? It would seem that the damage is done. Jesus gives the reason: "I am going to wake him up." In other words, instead of rushing off in response to the sisters' urgent summons to come to heal Lazarus, as Jesus had healed so many others, he delays until Lazarus is dead, then goes off to Bethany to raise him from the grave. How shocking!

Would Jesus deliberately have let a person die? One recent commentator, George Beasley-Murray,[1] believes that this is not the correct way to understand the story. He argues that Jesus does not delay in order to give Lazarus time to die, but only in order to allow him to be in the tomb for four days, which was the length of time required to make it clear that Lazarus' death was irreversible. He reasons that it would have taken a messenger one day to go from Bethany to where Jesus was, across the Jordan, in order to tell Jesus about Lazarus' illness. If Jesus spent two days delaying and then another day getting to Bethany, the total time, including the trip of the messenger, would add up to the four days Lazarus had been in the tomb when Jesus arrived. Conclusion: Lazarus must have died while the messenger was on his way to Jesus, and Jesus must have known that he was dead by the time the messenger arrived. Jesus' delay was for the purpose of filling out the four days required for the death to be irreversible. He did not delay in order to allow Lazarus to die.

That sounds like a reasonable argument, and it relieves Jesus of responsibility for Lazarus' death due to neglect. But there are some things against Beasley-Murray's line of reasoning. First, at several points in his gospel the Evangelist tells us when Jesus had some special knowledge (see 13:1, 3; 18:4; 19:28). If Jesus had special knowledge about Lazarus, why does the Evangelist not say so here? Indeed, why does he say something that flatly contradicts the suggestion that he did? In 11:6 he says, "when he heard that Lazarus was ill, he stayed in the place where he was for two days," not "since he knew that Lazarus was already dead."

The second point to be made against Beasley-Murray's exoneration of Jesus is that, if Jesus delayed in order to allow Lazarus to die, he is acting very much as he does elsewhere in the Fourth Gospel. In 2:4; 7:8-9; and 13:36, Jesus makes it clear that his calendar does not coincide with that of other human beings. What Jesus does is determined not by people's desires and needs but by what he sees his Father doing (5:19, 30; 8:28). Also, Jesus' actions frequently offend people (6:66; 13:8). The whole Gospel assures us that what Jesus does he does in order to bring life to human beings. But the way he goes about it is often out of step and even on a collision course with the immediate needs and standards of human beings. Throughout John's entire Gospel, Jesus challenges his listeners not to be offended by him.

Oddly, if Jesus' behavior in this story seems inexcusable to us, it also helps make this story very true to life. Have you ever prayed for God to come and deliver someone you loved who was in great danger? Did you ever do so in the confidence that this person was also for some reason especially dear to God? Did you ever do that and fail to get from God the response you desired?

From one end of the Bible to the other, at the beginning of Exodus, in the psalms, in the prophets, and in the Book of Revelation, people find themselves in the midst of calamity, and lament God's failure to rescue them. Since there are numerous indications in the Fourth Gospel that the Evangelist's own community was also suffering persecution and perhaps even dying for their faith, it is likely that they, too, were crying out to God for not responding to their urgent need.

Jesus' shocking behavior here is true to many people's experience of God. Because of this, we join Martha and Mary in crying out to Jesus, "Lord, if you had been here, my brother would not have died!"

Disappointment with Jesus

In Scene 3 Martha is very upset with Jesus when he finally does arrive. Her words to him are full of reproach. Her readiness to take Jesus to task here in John is very much in keeping with the way Luke portrays her in Luke 10:38-42: "Lord, is it of no concern to you that my sister has left me to serve by myself? So tell her to help me!"

Martha speaks for those of us who don't take God's failure to do what we want sitting down. Having taken Jesus to task for not preventing her brother's death, she blurts out, "But even now I know that God will give you whatever you ask of him." She refuses to accept the situation as it is. She wants something done to change it.

Jesus' response to Martha is, "Your brother will rise again." We know from an earlier scene in which Martha was not present that Jesus has come to Bethany to awaken Lazarus (v. 11). But Martha does not know Jesus' intention. And so she snaps back impatiently, "I know that he will rise again—in the resurrection at the last day!" Martha has misunderstood Jesus. But because she has misunderstood, she voices our own expectations and feelings. We, too, have been taught that those we have loved will rise at the resurrection of the last day. Jesus promises this repeatedly in his conversation with those who ate bread and fish by the Sea of Tiberius (6:39, 40, 44, 54). We try to believe it. But how satisfactory is that prospect as we stand beside the grave? Are we impatient, even angry, at the promises of God for the distant future? Why does God not do something to satisfy our longing right now?

When Mary goes out to meet Jesus, she repeats Martha's expression of disappointment at Jesus' failure to answer her urgent summons. But Mary speaks for us, not when we rebel against what God has allowed to happen to us, but when we are broken by it. She does nothing else but fall at Jesus' feet and weep.

It is in the context of these feelings that the Fourth Evangelist tells the story of Jesus raising Lazarus from the tomb. It is the context of God's love for us but apparent unresponsiveness to our urgent prayers in distress. It is the context of our feelings of disappointment, anger, brokenness as the result of what has happened. It is the context of present dissatisfaction with the promise that we and those we love will live again at the resurrection of the last day.

Experiencing Jesus' Power

But what does the story do for us beyond echoing or evoking the way we feel in the face of death? Does it promise that Jesus will *in this life* raise our loved ones from the dead as he raised Lazarus? Surely not! Few people besides Mary and Martha in Jesus' time had their faith in Jesus rewarded in such a way. No one today expects that this miracle will be repeated for them.

What, then, does the story of the raising of Lazarus offer? Does it in any way bring us beyond our own Martha-like impatience with Jesus' promise of the last day? The answer is most likely to be found in these words:

I am the resurrection and the life.
Those who believe in me,
even though they die,
will live,

and everyone who lives and believes in me
will never die. (vv. 25-26)

These words make it clear that faith in Jesus leads to more than
resurrection on the last day. Faith brings the life that shall never
end into the present. Before he raised Lazarus, Jesus often spoke of
eternal life as the believer's present possession (3:36; 5:24; 6:47,
54; 10:28). Once he said pointedly that the believer "has passed
from death to life" (5:24).

The raising of Lazarus is thus a sign like the miracle of the loaves
and fish. It is a physical miracle that points to a spiritual miracle.
In John 6, Jesus insists that the people not see in his power with
the loaves and fish a sign that he intended to fill their bellies with
physical bread. They must see his power to give them food for
their spirits, food that will fill them even now with eternal life. So
also in chapter 11 the raising of Lazarus does not mean that Jesus
will restore our loved ones to physical life. Rather, it seeks to draw
us into a world where we can experience Jesus' power to raise the
dead, and come to see in it a sign. If we believe Jesus is the
resurrection and the life, we will *now* begin to live a life that will
never die.

This is Jesus' answer to our disappointment and grief in the face
of death. He will not prevent death or immediately restore physical
life, but he gives the power of indestructible living in the face of
death. While few believers portrayed in the New Testament other
than Mary and Martha have had their dead restored to physical life,
countless have known the power of Jesus to fill their lives on this
side of death as though with water "gushing up to eternal life."
Through faith they have truly lived in spite of disappointment and
grief. They have lived confident in Jesus' promise that their coming
death does not make their present living futile. They do so because
they trust that the life that will lead to their death will never die.

What Sort of God?

But the story of Lazarus does more than point us to Jesus' power
to give never-ending life in the face of disappointment, grief, and
the fear of death. It also mediates an experience of God. Who is
the God revealed to us in Jesus Christ through this story?

At the beginning of the story, Jesus showed himself to be a person capable of love and intimate relationships, yet very independent in his response to the things others asked and expected of him. If he delayed going to Bethany to heal Lazarus, it was not because he didn't care about Lazarus and his sisters. On the contrary, he loved them. It was just that what he had in mind to do for Lazarus was not what Mary and Martha had in mind. They wanted Lazarus not to die; Jesus wanted him to rise from the dead.

What is your experience with God? Has God always given you what you asked for? If not, how did you understand what God was doing? This story shows us a God who, out of love, can refuse to respond to our prayers as well as give us what we desire. It shows us a God who will let us suffer greatly, but with a view to giving us something even greater than what we asked for. It shows us a God who rules over death, not just by restoring the dead to life, but by permitting death within the larger purpose of giving us real life. To use a modern concept, we might say that Jesus shows God to be a God who exercises tough love.

"Tough love" is love that permits a loved one to suffer. People who practice it believe that in the suffering the person will find what he or she really needs. But more than this, the person who shows tough love must endure the suffering and the reproach of the loved one for not "helping" in the way the person has asked. In Jesus' encounters with Martha and Mary, he does not just permit their suffering; he suffers along with them. Jesus listens to and suffers Martha's reproach. He does not reprimand her for it. He simply tells her what he is going to do. When she misunderstands and reacts with impatience, he does not try to show her that she has really misunderstood. He simply declares to her his power over death and asks her to trust him. Similarly, when he sees Mary and those with her weeping, he is moved first to anger and agitation and then to sharing their grief.

The New Revised Standard Version of the Bible (NRSV) translates the Evangelist's description of Jesus' feelings in verse 33 as "greatly disturbed in spirit and deeply moved." Most English translations and the standard dictionary of New Testament Greek have something similar. But in other biblical passages where we find the first verb, it means to admonish (Matt. 9:30; Mark 1:43), or to rebuke or become indignant (Dan. 11:30 in Greek; Mark

14:5). So it is better to translate it "became angry in spirit," as George Beasley-Murray does in a new commentary on John.[2]

What provokes Jesus' inner feeling of anger? He is angry at the power of death, which causes grief. Jesus is not, as some interpreters have argued, angry because those who weep lack faith in him. These mourners have just arrived at the place outside the village where Jesus was, and Mary has fallen at his feet and expressed her anguished disappointment at Jesus' failure to arrive in time to help. Jesus has said nothing to them about what he is about to do. And so it cannot be their lack of faith that moves him to anger. It is death!

In the Fourth Gospel death is always the cause of the second feeling attributed to Jesus in verse 33: "deeply moved," but better translated "agitated, shaken." See especially 12:27, where Jesus knows his coming death is for the glory of God, so he will not pray to be delivered from it. But its prospect does "shake" him ("troubled," NRSV). Jesus' own weeping (in 11:35) is also a response to death. He loved Lazarus, as some of the mourners rightly observe. When about to make his way to the tomb, he is moved to join them in their weeping.

Is Jesus' anger and grief in the face of death inconsistent with his intention to raise Lazarus from the dead and bring glory to himself and God? Surely not. Even though death and grief will end, till they do they are real and cause pain. When a mother exercising tough love allows a teenager to suffer, she trusts that when the suffering ends the child will be the better for it; but the future benefit does not prevent her from sharing the child's present pain.

What are your experiences of tough love? Have you been on either the giving or receiving end of it? If your own experience has taught you to value it, perhaps you can understand Jesus' decision in this story to delay, to allow his beloved friend Lazarus to die. And in the future when you pray and find your prayers unanswered, perhaps you will remember this story together with your own experience of tough love. May that memory nourish your faith that God rules even in your suffering and that through it or in spite of it, God is even now creating in you a life that will endure forever.

The Suffering of God

The Lazarus story, then, mediates an experience of God. And the God we encounter in Jesus is a God who loves us, who will act so that our sickness does not end in death, who is not controlled by our immediate feeling of need: a God who disappoints us, suffers our reproach, shares our grief. But God does something more yet. *God suffers the very suffering God permits us to suffer.* Here we must look at where the story of the death and resurrection of Lazarus really ends and at its role in John's entire Gospel.

Lists of stated readings for the church year, called lectionary lists, often call for the reading of the story of Lazarus during Lent. Of the lectionary lists I have checked, only one directs the reader to go beyond verse 44 or 45. And I myself have never heard anyone read beyond verse 44.

But the story begun in John 11:1-44 is incomplete without verses 45-53. First of all, verses 45 and 46 report the response of the witnesses to Jesus' great miracle. It is a divided response. Some as a result believe in Jesus; others go off and report Jesus' miracle to the Pharisees (a group of religious leaders who have been in open conflict with Jesus ever since John 7 and who have been party to the attempt to arrest him). This report to the Pharisees is the occasion for the meeting of the Sanhedrin, the ruling Jewish council, and the immediate response to Jesus' raising of Lazarus (vv. 47-53). How can we possibly end the story before we allow the Evangelist to report the response! And how dare we end the story, as one lectionary says to do, by reporting the positive response of verse 45 without the negative of verses 46 through 53!

The second reason that verses 45 through 53 are needed to complete the story of Lazarus is that the decision of the religious authorities to have Jesus killed brings us full circle, back to Jesus' conversation with his disciples near the beginning of the story (vv. 7-13). There the disciples object to returning to Judea because the last time Jesus was there the Judeans tried to stone him. If the story begins by sounding the note of danger in returning to Judea, it is incomplete until we find out if the disciples' fears are well-founded. And they are. Jesus' enemies gather in counsel, and their decision to get rid of Jesus reaches a new level of urgency and determination.

Do they get him? The question is unanswered unless we go on to the final scene of the story, verse 54. There we learn that, despite their new level of determination, the Pharisees and the chief priests will be delayed in carrying out their decision. Before they can do anything, Jesus' exits from Bethany and the territory of the Judeans.

What do we learn when we continue with John's story beyond the miraculous raising of a dead man to the results of that deed for Jesus' own life? We learn that Jesus' love for us is so tough that he is willing to perform this great sign of his power over death even at the cost of bringing about his own death. If he permits Lazarus to die so that he can raise him as a sign of his power over death, such suffering is no less than Jesus himself will shortly endure in order to rise as an even greater sign of his power to give eternal life.

Conclusion

The story of Lazarus, then, does not just promise resurrection. It also takes seriously our experience of death and grief. It speaks to that experience by bringing us into the presence of Jesus, the Son of God. Jesus indeed has the power to raise the dead but permits our physical death, shares our grief, endures our disappointment and reproach, and calls us to begin to live now a life that will never end. Perhaps we will be more willing to accept this exercise of "tough love" because the cost was not cheap. It came at the price of laying down his own life, of accepting the very death that he permits us to suffer.

Chapter Four

The Struggle for Justice
Pilate
John 18:28–19:16

Scene 1. Pilate and the Jewish Leaders Outside

18:28 Then they led Jesus from Caiaphas to Pilate's headquarters. It was early in the morning. They themselves did not enter the headquarters, so as to avoid ritual defilement and to be able to eat the Passover.

29 So Pilate went out to them and said, "What accusation do you bring against this man?" 30 They answered, "If this man were not an evildoer, we would not have handed him over to you!"

31 Pilate said to them, "Take him yourselves and judge him according to your law." The Jews replied, "We are not permitted to put anyone to death." 32 (This was to fulfill what Jesus had said when he indicated the kind of death he was to die.)

Scene 2. Pilate and Jesus Inside

33 Pilate entered the headquarters again, summoned Jesus, and asked him, "Are you the King of the Jews?" 34 Jesus answered, "Do you say this on your own, or did others tell you about me?" 35 Pilate replied, "I am not a Jew, am I? Your own nation and the chief priests have handed you over to me. What have you done?"

36 Jesus answered, "My kingdom is not from this world. If my kingdom were from this world, my followers would be fighting to keep me from being handed over to the Jews. But as it is, my kingdom is not from here." 37 Pilate asked him, "So you are a king?"

Jesus answered, "You say that I am a king. For this I was born, and for this I came into the world, to testify to the truth. Everyone

51

who belongs to the truth listens to my voice." [38] Pilate asked him, "What is truth?"

Scene 3. Pilate and the Jewish Leaders Outside

After he had said this, he went out to the Jews again and told them, "I find no case against him. [39] But you have a custom that I release someone for you at the Passover. Do you want me to release for you the King of the Jews?"

[40] They shouted in reply, "Not this man, but Barabbas!" Now Barabbas was a terrorist.

Scene 4. The Soldiers and Jesus Inside

[1] Then Pilate took Jesus and had him flogged. [2] And the soldiers wove a crown of thorns and put it on his head, and they dressed him in a purple robe. [3] They kept coming up to him, saying, "Hail, King of the Jews!" and striking him on the face.

Scene 5. Pilate and the Jewish Leaders Outside

[4] Pilate went out again and said to them, "Look, I am bringing him out to you to let you know that I find no case against him." [5] So Jesus came out, wearing the crown of thorns and the purple robe.

Pilate said to them, "Behold, the man!" [6] When the chief priests and the police saw him, they shouted, "Crucify him! Crucify him!"

Pilate said to them, "Take him yourselves and crucify him; I find no case against him." [7] The Jews answered him, "We have a law, and according to that law he ought to die because he has made himself the Son of God!"

Scene 6. Pilate and Jesus Inside

[8] When Pilate heard this, he was more afraid than ever. [9] He entered his headquarters again and asked Jesus, "Where are you from?" But Jesus gave him no answer.

[10] Pilate therefore said to him, "Do you refuse to speak to me? Do you not know that I have power to release you, and power to crucify you?" [11] Jesus answered him, "You would have no power over me unless it had been given you from above; therefore the one who handed me over to you is guilty of greater sin."

Scene 7. Pilate and the Jewish Leaders Outside

[12] From then on Pilate sought to release him, but the Jews cried out, "If you release this man, you are no friend of Caesar's. Everyone who claims to be a king sets himself against Caesar."

[13] When Pilate heard these words, he brought Jesus outside and sat on the judge's bench at a place called The Stone Pavement, or in Hebrew, Gabbatha. [14] Now it was the day of Preparation for the Passover; and it was about noon.

He said to the Jews, "Here is your King!" [15] They cried out, "Away with him! Away with him! Crucify him!"

Pilate said to them, "Shall I crucify your King?!" The chief priests answered, "We have no king but Caesar!" [16] Then he handed him over to them to be crucified.

Out of Step with the World

Ned was in his 90s when I got to know him. In the 1930s he had worked as the mechanic in charge of the delivery trucks for an ice cream company. He found many ways to save the company repair costs, and he hired the sharpest mechanics he could find.

One day Ned decided it was time to ask for a raise, not for himself, but for the men who were working for him. They were doing a top-notch job and had saved the company a lot of money in time and materials. Ned made an appointment to see the company president and presented to him his case for a raise.

"Come back tomorrow," the president answered. The next day Ned returned. The president was sitting behind his desk, and an enormous ledger was lying open on it. "Come here and look at this," the president said. "Do you see this column of figures?" he asked Ned. "Yes," Ned responded, "those are the expenses for my fleet of trucks." "Right," said the president, "those are the expenses for your fleet of trucks. You and your mechanics are a necessary evil in the operation of our company. There will be no raise for the men in your department!"

Ned was aghast. He took a few moments to collect his wits: then he recovered enough to speak. "Well, sir," he said, "if what I and my mechanics are doing is a necessary evil, then you have my resignation." And he walked out and never returned.

The story of Jesus in the Gospel of John is a story of a human being who obeyed God, not human beings, even when there was a heavy price to pay for being out of step. In hearing Jesus' story, many persons throughout history have come to know him and have been filled with his Spirit. They have heard the rhythm of his music, danced a different dance—and stepped on a lot of toes! Ned is one of those people. I know others. And their lives are a call to me to pray for the courage to follow Jesus along a different path.

In the Middle of Someone Else's Fight

In John's story of Jesus' trial before Pilate, the disruption Jesus causes by doing things his own way comes to a head. John's version of this story is considerably longer and more dramatic than the versions of the other Evangelists. Like the stories of the Samaritan woman and the blind man, the story of Pilate consists of seven scenes. The setting alternates between being outside Pilate's residence (the praetorium) and inside. The Jewish leaders remain outside, and for most of the story Jesus is inside, except when Pilate brings him out twice. As Pilate goes in and out, back and forth between the two locations, the tension builds. He is caught between the unrelenting pressure from the Jewish leaders to execute Jesus, on the one hand, and a growing conviction of Jesus' innocence and spiritual power, on the other.

Scene 1

As the story opens, the hostility is thick. The Jewish leaders have brought Jesus to Pilate, and they need Pilate's cooperation if they are to have Jesus put to death. Their strategy, however, does not augur success. Pilate is well known for his contempt for Jewish religious scruples. And they get off on the wrong foot from the very outset by refusing to defile themselves by setting foot inside his residence. If the Jewish leaders get what they want from Pilate, it will be by sheer determination.

Josephus, the Jewish historian who was a contemporary of Jesus, tells a story of a similar struggle between the Jews and Pilate.

> Now Pilate, the procurator of Judaea, . . . took a bold step in subversion of the Jewish practices, by introducing into the city [Jerusa-

lem] the busts of the emperor that were attached to the military standards, for our law forbids the making of images. . . . But when the people discovered it, they went in a throng to Caesarea and for many days entreated him to take away the images. He refused to yield . . .; however, since they did not cease entreating him, on the sixth day he secretly armed and placed his troops in position, while he himself came to the speaker's stand. . . . When the Jews again engaged in supplication, at a pre-arranged signal he surrounded them with his soldiers and threatened to punish them at once with death if they did not put an end to their tumult and return to their own places. But they, casting themselves prostrate and baring their throats, declared that they had gladly welcomed death rather than make bold to transgress the wise provisions of the laws. Pilate, astonished at the strength of their devotion to the laws, straightway removed the images from Jerusalem and brought them back to Caesarea.[1]

The Jewish leaders in John's narration not only offend this unsympathetic Roman governor by refusing to enter his residence; they have no legal basis for their demand that he execute Jesus. Pilate challenges them: "What accusation do you bring against this man?" They yell back: "If this man were not an evil doer, we would not have handed him over to you!" In contrast to the other Evangelists, John records (John 18:19–24) a hearing before the Jewish high priest that yields no criminal charge of any kind.

The Jewish leaders thus first offend Pilate and then demand he approve Jesus' execution with no legal justification. Pilate could end this whole matter immediately by refusing even to hear such a case. But he agrees to hear it anyway. And that is the beginning of this well-known and very pitiful chapter in the story of Roman justice.

John has devoted an entire scene to the Jewish leaders' efforts to get Pilate to consider their demand to kill Jesus. At the close of the scene John turns to us, his listeners, with a comment that leaves us in no doubt that Pilate will eventually do what the Jewish leaders demand: "This was to fulfill what Jesus had said when he indicated the kind of death he was to die." But how will the Jewish leaders bring Pilate around to doing their will? What will they do to persuade him?

Scene 2

During Pilate's first interrogation of Jesus, things go badly for the Jewish leaders' case. Pilate comes to the conclusion that Jesus is innocent of any punishable crime.

As in the other Gospels, Pilate opens with the question, "Are you the king of the Jews?" But in John his tone of voice is different. In Matthew, Mark, and Luke, he is saying, *Are* you the king of the Jews—as your leaders say you claim to be? In Mark 14:61-62 and Matthew 26:63-64, Jesus acknowledges before the high priest that he is the Messiah—a title with royal as well as other associations. [2] And in Luke 23:2, the leaders accuse Jesus before Pilate of "saying that he himself is the Messiah, a king." But in John, Jesus makes no such admission to the high priest, and the leaders make no such accusation before Pilate! And so in John Pilate's tone is the tone of a guess: "Are you [perhaps] the King of the Jews?"

Jesus' response in John is to seize the initiative. He replies to Pilate's question with a question of his own. Jesus' question contains the same words as his reply to Pilate in Matthew, Mark, and Luke. But instead of closing off any potential conversation with an acquiescent "*You say*," as in the other Gospels, Jesus sets off a defensive reaction in Pilate by asking, "Do *you say* this on your own, or did others tell you about me?" In the first half of his question Jesus is having some fun at Pilate's expense. He is speaking tongue in cheek. Is Pilate himself entertaining the possibility that Jesus may be a king? The implication of Jesus' question is ludicrous!

Pilate catches and responds to the implication immediately. "Am I a Jew?!" he blurts out with derisive laughter. But Jesus has asked a very telling question. Pilate laughs out of court the suggestion that he came up with the possibility of Jesus' kingship on his own. But if he didn't come up with it on his own, where did it come from? Had others been telling him about Jesus? In fact, no one told Pilate that Jesus was claiming to be king. Not in John's story they didn't! So he *must* have come up with the accusation on his own.

In asking his question, Pilate appears simply to be making a reasonable guess. He was an official of the Roman government, responsible for keeping the peace in the capital of a nation that continually celebrated its liberation from Egyptian slavery and was ripe for revolt. Pilate was on the lookout for local leaders who might pose a threat to Roman rule by claiming to be king.

However, while Pilate may have his own reasons for asking if Jesus is fancying himself a king, he ironically guesses the truth. And according to John, human beings do not do and say what is true of their "own accord." It is God who prompts them. Preeminently, God prompts Jesus' works and teaching (5:19; 7:17, 18, 28; 8:28, 42; 14:10). But God also prompts the Spirit to guide Jesus' disciples into all the truth (16:13) and ironically prompts the high priest to prophesy of Jesus' death and its meaning (11:50-51). The only exception is that Jesus lays down his life "of my own accord" (10:18). But even so he does it on command of his Father.

Jesus' question to Pilate is itself filled to the brim with irony. Like Caiaphas, who unintentionally spoke for God when he prophesied that Jesus would die for the nation (John 11:50-52), Pilate unintentionally bears witness to the truth that Jesus is king of the Jews. At this point in the interrogation, Pilate is scornful of any suggestion that he might think Jesus actually is king of the Jews. But by the end of the story, Pilate's witness to Jesus' kingship will develop into something akin to the confession of the centurion in Mark 15:39.

After his derisive retort to Jesus' question, Pilate retreats from guessing at an accusation and gets back to the facts of what the Jewish leaders actually did and said. He had asked them what accusation they were bringing against Jesus and they had retorted, "If this man were not an evil*doer*, we would not have *handed him over to you*." Now Pilate points out to Jesus, "Your own nation and chief priests have *handed you over to me*. What have you *done?*" And even though the Jewish leaders did not accuse him of claiming to be a king, Jesus answers Pilate's question in terms of kingship.

To anyone who has been listening to John tell his Gospel story from the very beginning, and has been listening attentively, the idea that Jesus is king of the Jews is familiar, although somewhat ambiguous. Near the beginning Nathanial declared that Jesus is "King of Israel" (1:49). Later, when the people witnessed Jesus' miracle of feeding the five thousand by the Sea of Galilee, they wanted to take him by force and make him their king. But Jesus got away by himself (6:15). Later yet, when on a donkey's colt he entered Jerusalem for the Passover, the people hailed him as "King of Israel" (12:12–16). There is truth, then, in Pilate's God-inspired guess that Jesus may be claiming to be king of the Jews. No wonder Jesus responds to Pilate's question "What have you done?" in terms of kingship. But there is both a positive and negative side to what he says about it. "My kingdom"—he begins, acknowledging that he is a king—"is not from this world"—he continues, qualifying the nature of his kingship.

What does Jesus mean by declaring "My kingdom is *not from this world*"? Does he mean he exercises no rule whatever in this world? Clearly not! According to John, Jesus is the light of the world (3:19); he exercises judgment in the world (9:39); and through his death he will cast out the ruler of this world and draw all people to himself (12:27–33). What Jesus does mean he makes clear in the words that follow. He first qualifies his meaning negatively: "If my kingdom were from this world, my followers would be fighting to keep me from being handed over to the Jews." In other words, his way of exercising his kingship is not the way of violence practiced by the world. Stated positively, Jesus exercises his not-from-this-world kingship by bearing witness to the truth and by successfully communicating with those who are of the truth: They hear his voice. This is not a rejection of the idea of kingship. The words "listens to my voice" echo Jesus' words about the Good Shepherd in John 10:16. The image of the shepherd is a kingly image. King David was a shepherd. The rulers of Israel are sometimes called shepherds in the Old Testament. But Jesus exercises his kingship by bearing witness to the truth and by laying down his life for the sheep, not by using violence. Human beings in this world are left free to accept or to reject his kingship. Only those who "belong to the truth" are ruled by Jesus in this world.

Is the story of the Christian church the story of a people who have lived obeying Jesus as king? To our great shame and grief, Christians individually and as the institutional church have, on the whole, rejected Jesus' peculiar form of kingship. We have rejected it particularly in our relationship with the Jews. Incredibly this very passion story, in which Jesus explicitly and later graphically, rejects the use of violence even in self-defense, has from time to time throughout Christian history helped inflame hatred in the hearts of people who claimed Christ as their king. Jews in Europe hid behind locked doors on Good Friday because on that day when the entire passion narrative from John was read in the churches, they were vulnerable to threats and violence from Christians. [3]

The result is that it is the Jews, not the Christians, who throughout most of the last two thousand years rejected the way of violence and lived as though Jesus was their king, even if they did not acclaim him king. They boldly lived according to what they believed to be the truth, even though they often lost their lives for doing so. They did so with few incidents of organized effort to fight back with violence.

There is great irony in Jesus' kingship over the Jews who verbally rejected it and the betrayal of Jesus' kingship by those followers who verbally professed it. The resulting Holocaust in this century has given the Jews tremendous moral power while stripping it from the church. However, the modern state of Israel has revolted in both feelings and policies against the way Jews for centuries refused to defend themselves.

An increasing number of modern Christians are appalled at the way Christians throughout history have used the Pilate narrative and other stories from the New Testament as an excuse for violence against Jews. Some theologians even advocate a moratorium on the reading of such New Testament stories in Christian worship. It is unrealistic to think that Christian congregations will stop reading this story. But we must devote ourselves to helping people hear its true challenge!

Clearly, we Christians must stop merely professing Jesus' kingship; we must start *living* Jesus' kingship, particularly in our relationship with Jews. We must refrain from all derogatory language about Jews. Even more, we must come to know and appreciate Jews and Judaism. With prejudicial words we clearly forfeit our right to proclaim Jesus' kingship to Jews with words. The only way open to us is to proclaim it with our lives.

Scene 3

Pilate's parting words to Jesus at the end of scene 2 were a cynical "What is truth?" That is a question echoed again and again in our pluralistic culture, often with as much cynicism as Pilate's. But despite our general cynicism, each of us has at least a few pet issues on which we have very strong convictions. Pilate has some clear convictions too. He is quite certain about truth when it comes to the question of Jesus' guilt or innocence. Jesus is not guilty of a crime! And Pilate goes out to the Jewish leaders to pronounce his verdict.

But Pilate has another agenda in addition to his desire that justice prevail. He is eager that all parties involved in this matter should win. He wants very much to release Jesus, but he also wants the Jewish leaders to give his action their blessing. So he offers them a way to go along with his decision without looking bad: They can agree to Jesus' release in accordance with their own custom!

Note that in Matthew and Mark it is the crowd that comes up to Pilate during the feast of Passover and demands that he follow this custom. In John's story, however, it is Pilate who brings this custom into play as a way of mollifying the Jewish leaders. (Luke makes no mention of the custom at all. In the King James Version, Luke notes the custom in 23:17. But a NRSV footnote shows that this explanation was added by early copyists when they discovered it was missing from Luke's story.)

But according to John the Jewish leaders will not be moved. They shout back, "Not this fellow, but Barabbas!" John closes this scene with the comment, "Now Barabbas was a . . . " A what?

The RSV says, "Now Barabbas was a robber"; the Good News Bible and the New Revised Standard Version call him a "bandit"; and the NIV paraphrases the word by saying, "Barabbas had taken part in a rebellion." The word being translated in these different ways is the Greek word *lestes*. The best translation here is "terrorist." It was used as a label for some of the groups and individuals who fought the Romans in the Jewish War of A.D. 66-70 and who in the process often robbed and terrorized their own people to accomplish their ends. Mark and Luke both tell us that Barabbas was in prison for murder and insurrection. This same Greek word also recalls Jesus' earlier address to the Jewish leaders in chapter 10. There Jesus applies the label *lestes* to one who, like a thief rather than like a shepherd, climbs over the wall of the sheepfold instead of going in through the door.

In demanding the release of Barabbas, the Jewish leaders are preferring a robber to a shepherd, a violent revolutionary to a shepherd-king. The shepherd commits no violence, but establishes his kingdom by witnessing to the truth and leading the flock who hear his voice. The Jews' preference for such a robber-revolutionary-terrorist would have tragic results for them. It was just such people who would lead an aborted revolution against Rome, which ended in the destruction of the Temple in Jerusalem and the end of the Jewish nation in A.D. 70. The Jews' persistence in wanting the release of Barabbas the revolutionary is also highly ironic because they claim in John 19:12 and 15 that it is Jesus who sets himself up as a rival to Caesar and that they, his accusers, have no king but Caesar.

Scene 3 summons us to some honest reflection. Once again we must ask ourselves, Is the story of the Christian church the story of people who have preferred Jesus to Barabbas? The story of Martin Luther King, Jr., and those who followed his leadership is the story of a few who did. The story of John Calvin's church in Geneva, Switzerland, is full of violence by Christian leaders against many people who disagreed with them. Each of us must ask ourselves, What is my response when matters about which I have strong convictions are at stake? Do I speak what I believe to be the truth and let the chips fall where they may? Or do I resort to subtle forms of coercion in an effort to prevail?

Scenes 4 and 5

Pilate's next strategy in his effort to release Jesus with the consent of the Jewish leaders is compromise. He will mete out at least some punishment. (Notice the very different role of the scourging in Matthew and Mark, where it is a prelude to execution. Notice, too, how in Luke 23:11 it is Herod's soldiers who carry it out, not Pilate's soldiers.) In John's story Pilate takes a new step down the path of injustice. He took the first step when he agreed to try Jesus without a specific charge. He took the second step by carrying out this undeserved punishment, albeit less severe than execution.

The Roman soldiers, however, do not just beat Jesus. As in all the other Gospels, they mock his claim to be a king. They robe

Jesus in purple, crown him with thorns, exclaim "Hail, king of the Jews!" and strike him. When in John they finish, they do not strip Jesus of the purple robe (as they do in Matthew and Mark) before they lead him out to crucify him. Pilate himself leads Jesus outside the praetorium to present him to the Jewish leaders. "Behold the man!" he says to them, in mock acclamation, not only of Jesus' claim but of the seriousness with which the Jewish leaders themselves take Jesus. The New American Bible translates Pilate's words, "Look at the man!" which suggests a tone of disdain rather than mock serious-ness. But it comes to the same thing. Pilate's intention is to persuade the Jewish leaders that such a pitiful person cannot be worth the fuss they are making about getting rid of him.

But who is truly pitiful in this scene? Is it Jesus, who suffers because of a deliberate choice to lay down his life? Or is it Pilate, whose desire to have everybody come up a winner renders him too weak to stand up for Jesus' innocence?

It was Palm Sunday in 1972. The Vietnam War still dragged on. All during the war people had been protesting in various ways and, like Jesus, paying the price by going to jail. I had just begun to serve a church in a small town in Pennsylvania. I wanted people to understand how the Jewish leaders must have felt about Jesus when he rode into Jerusalem on the donkey. And so I pointed out some similarities between Jesus and war protestors. In my sermon I was simply stating the truth as I saw it. One of the prominent members of the church, the father of a son in the United States Marines Corps in Vietnam, had some choice words to say about me the following week. I for my part had been more naive than courageous. If I had known about this man's son, I think I would have chosen to be more like Pilate and refrained from making such a comparison.

But it is not only in connection with issues of national significance that we are confronted with the choice between imitating Jesus or Pilate.

I once worked with an excellent church consistory president. When her four-year term as elder was up, the nominating committee offered her name for election to another term, so she could continue to serve as president. But during the election, someone nominated a rival from the floor, which was against all precedent, and this superb president was defeated.

After the election she told me that there was a small group of persons in the church who had planned her defeat a long time ago. To my great

*shame, I never went to the alleged conspirators to confront them with
what she told me.*

The Jewish leaders are not the least bit swayed by Pilate's effort
to appease them. What incenses them is not Jesus' claim to be
their king. They have made no mention of that. Their problem is
that "he has made himself the Son of God." Ever since chapter 5
their effort to put him to death for this claim has echoed through
the Gospel. In John 5:18, the Evangelist tells us that "the Jews
were seeking all the more to kill him, because he . . . was also
calling God his own Father, thereby making himself equal to God."
In 8:58–59, "they picked up stones to throw at him" because he
declared, "Very truly, I tell you, before Abraham was, I am." And
in 10:33 they say, "It is not for a good work that we are going to
stone you, but for blasphemy; because you, though only a human
being, are making yourself God."

The Jewish leaders did not accuse Jesus of claiming to be the
Son of God when they handed him over to Pilate for trial. As
much as that was a capital offense in Jewish law (19:7), it was not a
capital offense for pagan Romans. Indeed, their angry and frus-
trated outburst about it here has an effect on Pilate exactly the
opposite to the one they have been seeking.

Scene 6

All through the story of the trial, Pilate has been defending
Jesus' innocence. And Pilate's effort to appease the Jewish leaders
by beating Jesus and mocking him has borne ironic witness to
Jesus' kingship. Pilate's response to the report that Jesus makes
himself the Son of God brings Pilate's witness to a new level. He is
no longer merely impressed with Jesus' political innocuousness and
innocence. He is affected by Jesus' divine power.

There is a scene very much like this in a second century A.D.
biography of a first-century miracle worker named Apollonius of
Tyana. According to it, as Apollonius is traveling, he comes to a
frontier. Before he is allowed to cross it, he is brought before an
official of the king to be questioned.

> When he [the official] saw a man so dried up and parched
> [Apollonius], he began to bawl out like a cowardly woman and hid his
> face, and could hardly be induced to look up at him. "Whence do you

come to us?" he said, "and who sent you?" as if he was asking questions of a spirit. And Apollonius replied: "I have sent myself, to see whether I can make men of you, whether you like it or not." He asked a second time who he was to come trespassing like that into the king's country, and Apollonius said: "All the earth is mine, and I have a right to go all over it and through it." Whereupon the other said, "I will torture you, if you don't answer my questions." "And I hope," said the other, "that you will do it with your own hands, so that you may be tested by the touchstone of a true man." [4]

This scene from the *Life of Apollonius* contains some very interesting similarities to scene 6 of John's story of Jesus before Pilate. The official is afraid of Apollonius. He asks, "Whence do you come to us?" He threatens to torture Apollonius. And all the while Apollonius' response is one of confident authority. Rattled with fear Pilate asks Jesus, "Where are you from?" The question has been debated throughout the Gospel. Look up John 7:27-28; 8:14; 9:30; also, John the Baptist's witness to Jesus in 3:27, 31; and Jesus' discussion with Nicodemus about the origin of belief in Jesus in 3:3, 7, 8. In all these passages the Greek ending *-then*, meaning "from," sounds again and again. But when Pilate asks the question, Jesus remains silent. The Evangelist depends on those of us who have been listening to him to remember what had been said before and to draw our own conclusion.

Receiving no answer, Pilate tries exercising his authority. This time Jesus responds. He makes clear his view of who is really exercising authority over these proceedings. Pilate's only authority is what he has been given "from above." Jesus' reply also contains the answer to Pilate's earlier question, "Where are you from?" The answer is also "from above"!

The scene ends with Jesus' declaration that Pilate is exercising no more authority over Jesus than is granted by the source of Jesus' own authority. "Therefore," declares Jesus, "the one who handed me over to you is guilty of a greater sin." It is a common biblical theme beginning with the role of pharaoh in the story of the Exodus that, although God is in control of the saving events of history, those who oppose God are nonetheless guilty of sin. Who is "the one who handed me over to you"? The word "handed over" is the same word that is often translated "betrayed." It weaves its way through every Gospel. And as it moves along it gathers other names about itself: first Judas (6:64, 71; 12:4), then Satan in collusion with Judas (13:2), then Judas again (13:11, 21; 18:2, 5), then the Jewish leaders (18:30, 35, 36). And at the end of this story Pilate will add his own name to the list (19:16). Will we add our's also?

Scene 7

The conflict between Pilate and the Jewish leaders has reached a stalemate. The leaders have defeated every strategy of Pilate for securing their agreement to a release of Jesus. As for Pilate, he has moved from an initial antipathy to the Jewish leaders, to a conviction that Jesus is innocent, to fear of Jesus as a divine being.

John's next report is that Pilate "sought to release him." "Seeking" has characterized the effort of Jesus' opponents to arrest and kill him ever since the beginning of the controversies. (See 5:18, 7:1, 30; 10:39; 18:4, where the NRSV uses a variety of translations for the Greek word *zeteo*.) Pilate's effort to undo the leaders' success in bringing Jesus toward their goal has now risen to a level that matches theirs.

But the Jews are holding a high card they haven't played yet, and Pilate does not have the hand to beat it. Pilate has been unimpressed with the general accusation that Jesus is an evildoer, but he is filled with fear at the charge that he "has claimed to be the Son of God." How will Pilate react if the Jewish leaders point out the implications of Pilate's own presentation, albeit a mocking one, of Jesus as king? In other words, it is time for them to change strategies. Instead of attacking Jesus alone, it is time to attack Pilate as well: "If you release this man, you are no friend of Caesar! Everyone who claims to be a king sets himself against Caesar!"

All Pilate can do now is to make a show of his power. He brings the prisoner out and sits down on the judgment seat in order to deliver his verdict.

Before the Evangelist goes on, he informs us with great irony that it is the sixth hour of the day. This is the hour of the slaughter of the Passover lambs in the Temple in Jerusalem. It commemorates the escape of the Jews from oppression by the Egyptians. Do we recall John the Baptist's witness to Jesus at the beginning of the Gospel: "Here is the Lamb of God who takes away the sin of the world!"? John is inviting us to see Jesus here as the true Passover

lamb. Through his very death Jesus is the source of freedom for
the Jews, who now suffer under the domination of Rome as they
once suffered under the Egyptians. Indeed, all during his trial,
Jesus has shown himself to be the only one who is truly free.
Pilate now displays his power. It is hollow. He is interested in
vindicating himself, not in doing justice by Jesus. So instead of
exercising his authority as governor by pronouncing Jesus innocent
and releasing him, Pilate tries to secure his own innocence. "Here
is your King!" he says, ridiculing the idea that in releasing this
mocked and beaten Jesus he is releasing a serious threat to Caesar's
rule. But the Jewish leaders have found Pilate's Achilles' heel.
There is no reason for them to quit now. They confidently insist
on their original demand: "Away with him! Away with him!
Crucify him!" Pilate makes one final attempt at ridiculing them:
"Shall I crucify your King?!" It is the pathetic effort of a man who
is powerless for no other reason than that he is unwilling to pay the
price of standing up for what he believes. The chief priests twist
the sword with words that threaten to make them look like loyal
Romans and Pilate like a traitor: "We have no king but Caesar!"
And Pilate at last bows to their will.

That the Wicked Should Turn from Their Way and Live

As we come away from the trial story, what do we carry with us?
John surely hopes that we will be profoundly impressed by the
kingly bearing of Jesus. But how do we feel about Pilate and the
Jewish leaders? Are they villains who arouse our hatred, or are they
reflections of our own selves?

Christians throughout history have been inflamed by this story
with hatred for "the Jews," and with sympathy for Pilate as the
unfortunate victim of Jewish determination. Those feelings have
often boiled over into the persecution of defenseless Jews in the
name of one who rejected the use of violence even in self-defense
and have deluded the persecutors into thinking that they were
thereby "offering service to God" (John 16:2).

The history of Christian persecuion of the Jews teaches in a
dramatic way a lesson Christians must learn about our relationships with all peoples: We, like all other people, are very prone to

exercising our power unjustly and in our own self-interest, in blatant opposition to the rule of Jesus our Sovereign. If we have not persecuted Jews, have we nevertheless betrayed justice in order to increase our profits, protect ourselves from people of another race, maintain our popularity among our friends, and even guarantee that others will do what we believe is "right"? This story of Pilate, Jesus, and the Jewish leaders ought to serve as a challenge to all our natural tendencies to use power unjustly in our self-interest and even for our own self-preservation.

How do we move beyond seeing in Pilate and the Jewish leaders reflections of our own human weakness and readiness to betray justice? How can we be transformed into persons who are more like Jesus?

One way may be to hear this story in such a way that we relive that ancient event and sense being in Jesus' presence. Perhaps as we experience his presence through the story, we will be drawn to him and be filled with a desire to trust that he really is the Way, the Truth, and the Life (John 14:6). Beyond that we must pray for and rely on the transforming power of the Holy Spirit, that "blows where it chooses, and you hear the sound of it, but you do not know where it comes or where it goes" (John 3:8).

The Jews in the Fourth Gospel

According to John 19:6 and 15, the opponents of Jesus in the Pilate narrative are the chief priests and temple police, who had been sent by the Jewish leaders to arrest Jesus (see 7:32, 45–46; 18:3, 12). Yet Christians have characteristically laid responsibility for the death of Jesus at the door of "the Jews" and Judaism as a whole. This is partly because in the other three Gospels the Jewish crowds tipped the scales against Jesus by joining their leaders in demanding Jesus' execution. But it is also because John himself refers to the opponents of Jesus in the Pilate trial simply as "the Jews."

For this reason, as I have already pointed out, many stories from the Gospel of John are under attack from a number of Christian theologians today. Appalled by the Holocaust, these theologians believe that stories that label the opponents of Jesus simply as "the

Jews" help perpetuate this negative attitude towards Jews and Judaism. How, these theologians ask, can we continue to read such stories if prejudice is the result—especially when John's generalizing of Jewish guilt is a blatant, historical lie? Even if crowds of common people did join their leaders in demanding Jesus' death, as Matthew, Mark, and Luke say they did, they were still only a small group of Jesus' Jewish contemporaries!

This problem of responsibility for Jesus' death is very difficult to deal with in the New Testament. Attending to it may offer insight into relationships between other groups as well as between Christians and Jews.

It is important to recognize that such generalizing when labeling people is common today within many autonomous groups. Using "them" and "us" places the blame for what a group believes to be wrong. While more and more Christians rightly shrink from condemning the Jews for the death of Jesus, many readily pronounce judgment upon "the church," "Americans," "Western culture," "WASPS" and "men" for one form of evil or another. Obviously, not all persons to whom these labels apply are guilty of the evil laid at their door, and many labeled people have actively worked to correct injustices. Yet the blanket accusations continue. Why?

One reason is that those who use generalized language are often members of an oppressed group who speak forcefully in order to call members of the offending group to accountability. The language summons *all* members of the oppressing group to cease from contributing actively to oppression, to desist from supporting it in any way. The victims are sometimes joined in their general condemnation by members of the very group being condemned! Whites who protest white injustice against blacks, men who protest the injustice perpetrated by men upon women, for example, take up the cry of the sufferers, often employing the same generalized language as an expression of their alienation from their own group.

Sometimes this use of generalized language is justified, for we participate in what is done in our name if we do not speak out against it. If what is done in our name is evil, justice calls us to do what we can to oppose that evil.

But not all generalizing condemnations are justified! It is one thing to pronounce judgment upon the members of an oppressing group and to call to repentance those who perpetrate, support, and fail to protest it. It is quite another thing to continue to condemn the group long after their oppressive actions have ceased or to viciously turn the tables on the former offenders, as the Christian church did on the Jews.

We Christians who have heard in the Fourth Evangelist's story "The Jews versus Jesus and His Followers" must hear the even more painful story "Jesus' Followers versus Jesus and the Jews." In the greatest betrayal of Jesus imaginable, we followers of Jesus have stood John's story on its head! In the story "The Jews versus Jesus and His Followers" we must learn to hear other stories in which our group as a whole, and therefore we ourselves, either perpetrate or suffer injustice. When we learn to hear the story in new and more truthful ways, we may experience a new and more powerful encounter with the risen but still suffering Christ. May that encounter be a transforming encounter. May we as persecutors be confronted by Jesus through this new story, as Saul was confronted by Jesus on the way to Damascus through a vision. May we too be converted from persecutors into persons who share Christ's sufferings! And if we suffer injustice, may our encounter with Jesus through this story inspire us with loyalty to one whose power is of another order than the power of this world, yet whose power is truth.

Chapter Five

Grief Turned to Joy
Mary Magdalene

John 20:1–18 *(Author's Translation)*

Underlined words and phrases produce for the listener and reader a pattern of Mary's discoveries, from the disturbed stone to her resurrected Lord.

Act I

Scene 1. A Moved Stone

¹ Now on the first day of the week Mary Magdalene comes, early, while it is still dark, to the tomb, and she sees the <u>stone taken away</u> from the tomb! ² So she runs and she comes to Simon Peter and to the other disciple, the one Jesus loved, and she says to them, "They've taken the Lord out of the tomb, and we don't know where they've put him!"

Scene 2. Grave Cloths

³ So out went Simon Peter and the other disciple and they headed for the tomb. ⁴ Now the two began to run together, but the other disciple ran on ahead, faster than Peter, ⁵ and he came first to the tomb. And he bent down to look in, and he sees lying there— <u>the grave cloths</u>! But he didn't go in.

Scene 3. Face Cloth

⁶ Then along comes Simon Peter, too, following him. And he went into the tomb and he sees the grave cloths lying there, ⁷ and <u>the face cloth</u>, which was on his head, not lying with the grave cloths, but apart, rolled up in a place by itself.

Scene 4. Belief

⁸ So then the other disciple went in also, the one who came first to the tomb, and he saw, and he believed! ⁹ You see, they did not yet know the scripture that he must rise from the dead.

Act II

Scene 5. Grief

¹⁰ So the disciples went back home. ¹¹ But Mary stood at the tomb, outside, weeping.

Scene 6. Two Angels

¹² Now while she was weeping, she bent down to look into the tomb, and she sees <u>two angels</u> dressed in white sitting there, one at the head and one at the feet, where the body of Jesus had been lying. ¹³ And they say to her, "Woman, why are you weeping?" She says to them, "Because they took my Lord and I don't know where they put him."

Scene 7. The Gardener

¹⁴ Having said this, she turned around and sees <u>Jesus</u> standing there—and <u>she didn't know that it was Jesus</u>. ¹⁵ Jesus says to her, "Woman, why are you weeping? Who are you looking for?" She, thinking that he was the gardener, says to him, "Sir, if you have carried him away, tell me where you have put him, and I will take him."

Scene 8. Rabboni!

¹⁶ Jesus says to her, "Mary!" Turning she says to him in Hebrew, "<u>Rabboni!</u>" which means, "Teacher!"

Scene 9. Good News

¹⁷ Jesus says to her, "Do not hold me; for I have not yet ascended to the Father. But go to my brothers and tell them I am ascending to my Father and your Father, and my God and your God." ¹⁸ Mary Magdalene comes shouting the news to the disciples, "I have seen the Lord!" and that he said these things to her!

From Joy to Grief to Joy

Ten years ago my wife, Jane, and I moved to the beautiful farm country of southern Schuylkill County, Pennsylvania. We had bought eleven acres on the southern slope of a hill that looks out to the bird sanctuary Hawk Mountain. We came so that we could have our horses on our own property instead of ten miles away at a boarding stable. We bought three sheep to eat the poison ivy in our pastures. After years of living in cities and suburban neighborhoods, we basked in the beauty and peace of nature.

Three years later Jane began to have trouble with a tendon on her hand. She had an operation, but the incision wouldn't heal properly. One day while I was cleaning the stable, she came home from the doctor's to tell me she had been diagnosed with the early stages of a crippling, possibly fatal disease.

Suddenly the beauty of nature around me lost its glory. We had shared in more than fifteen years of marriage and in all we had put into our new little farm. I couldn't imagine my world without Jane. Day by day we watched for new symptoms to appear. After some time she went to a hospital for a few days of tests.

We had about four months of anxiety before we made a trip to Pittsburgh to see a specialist, a doctor who knew more about the beginning stages of the disease than anyone else. He examined her and questioned her for about an hour. Then she told me the verdict: the initial diagnosis had been wrong!

The world through which we drove home from Pittsburgh was a brand new world, bright and shining and full of joy. The linen grave cloths had been unwound from around my heart. The dearest person in my life had been restored to me. My grief had been turned to joy.

A Familiar Story

In John there are three stories of Jesus' appearances to his followers after his resurrection. All of them are well known and well loved because they exhibit John's characteristic vividness and drama.

The first of these three stories (John 20:11-18) is the story best remembered for the tender encounter between Mary Magdalene and the risen Jesus. You will recall that when she saw him she thought he was the gardener. When he said her name, she turned around and burst out in Hebrew, "Rabboni!" And then, according to the King James Version, he said to her, "Touch me not; for I am not yet ascended to my Father."

That encounter is the beautiful climax of a story that begins fifteen verses earlier and involves not only Mary Magdalene and Jesus but Peter and the beloved disciple as well. The story as a whole is a marvelous little work of narrative art.

Before you go any further, take time to read John 20:1-18 aloud. The translation at the beginning of this chapter arranges the text in a way that will help you to reproduce its movement in time. Be sure to pause between scenes. And be as dramatic as you are when you tell someone about an event in your own life that excites you.

As you read, you may find the language of my translation awkward and choppy. That is because it follows the Greek text virtually word for word and tense for tense. The language of the Greek text is the kind of language we speak in our everyday conversation, but it is not the kind of language we are used to reading. It is a challenge to read it in a way that sounds natural because its natural setting is not in the reading but in the excitement of the moment.

Two Waves of Discovery

In nine little movements of a few sentences each, John tells the story of the discovery of Jesus' resurrection. Together these nine movements create a drama in two acts of roughly equal length. The first four scenes (vv. 1-9) make up a first act, which begins with Mary Magdalene but quickly turns from her to Peter and the beloved disciple. The last five scenes (vv. 10-18) make up a second act, which turns back to Mary.

We shall see that these two acts are two waves of discovery. Verses 1 through 9 roll along until they peak and break when the beloved disciple realizes that Jesus must have risen from the dead. Then the water recedes, only to roll in once more, and peak and break when Mary encounters the risen Jesus himself.

The First Wave

The first act, or wave of discovery, begins when Mary Magdalene comes to the tomb in the wee hours of the morning. What she sees fills her with bewilderment and terror: The stone has been taken away from the tomb! In a panic she runs to Peter and the Beloved Disciple and frantically blurts out, "They've taken the Lord out of the tomb, and we don't know where they've put him!"

To appreciate Mary's experience here, dare to imagine visiting the grave of someone you have loved dearly only to find it disturbed by vandals. When Mary arrived at the tomb to mourn, that is what she thought had happened. Someone had moved the stone which had sealed the entrance to the tomb! There is no report that she looked inside the tomb at this point. She didn't need to look in. If the stone had been moved, someone had stolen the body!

Grave robberies were not unknown in the first century. A first-century imperial edict found on a marble slab at Nazareth reads thus:

> Ordinance of Caesar. It is my pleasure that graves and tombs remain undisturbed in perpetuity. . . . If however any man lay information that another has either demolished them, or has in any other way extracted the buried, or has maliciously transferred them to other places in order to wrong them, or has displaced the sealing or other stones . . . I desire that the offender be sentenced to capital punishment on charge of violation of sepulture." [1]

So Mary "runs and she comes . . . and she says." The verbs in the Greek text are in what we call the "historical present" tense. It is the tense we use in telling stories. It is the tense of excitement and vividness. It is the tense that makes a past event present. To make this story come alive for you, think of a time you were in a panic.

When I was about six years old, I was playing with a friend in the back yard. For some reason he started hitting me in the legs with a green florist stick. I turned around and picked a rusty file out of the trash can and threw it at him. I hit him right in the head! In a panic I flew into the house to tell my parents.

Mary, too, is off in a flash to get help from Jesus' two closest friends. "They've taken the Lord out of the tomb," she blurts out breathless, "and we don't know where they've put him!"

In scene 2 the focus switches to Peter and the Beloved Disciple. (Note that the Evangelist never calls the Beloved Disciple, John. The Evangelist is not interested in the disciple's name. He is interested in his relationship with Jesus, the fact that Jesus loved him.) When Mary arrives in a panic, they react to her news in the same way. "Out went Simon Peter and the other disciple," the Greek text reads. The all-important word of action comes first. And the verbs that follow sustain the atmosphere of alarm.

The Beloved Disciple does not wait for Peter to keep up with him. (Many people have concluded from this that the Beloved Disciple was therefore younger than Peter. But it is also possible that he was an older man but just a faster runner!) As he heads for the tomb, his concern is not for Peter but for getting to the tomb as fast as he can to find out what has happened.

The separation of the two disciples helps to create suspense. It also allows the Evangelist to unfold events in stages. With each stage the Evangelist reveals to us a little more.

First, the beloved disciple arrives at the tomb. He looks inside without actually entering. What does he see? In the order of the words in the Greek text, "he sees, lying there, the grave cloths!"

This report brings us a step beyond the discovery made by Mary. Mary did not look inside the tomb. She saw the stone moved from the entrance and that was all. When the Beloved Disciple arrives, he looks inside and to his amazement sees the grave cloths!

No one, as the fourth-century Greek theologian John Chrysostom remarked, would steal a body and leave the grave wrappings. Why not? Chrysostom does not tell us. We might guess that to unwrap the body would slow the robbers down, would make carrying the body more difficult. More likely, the primary cause of the robbery was to obtain the valuable linen cloths and the spices. To leave them behind would therefore make no sense! Remember that in John's story of Jesus' burial, he reported that Nicodemus and Joseph of Arimathea wrapped 100 pounds of myrrh and aloes—an enormous quantity!—into the linen grave cloths (John 19:39-40).

But even if Jesus' body had been unwrapped, that does not necessarily mean that it had been taken out of the tomb. So with the help of Peter, in scene 3 the Evangelist takes us inside the tomb to have a good look around. Through Peter's eyes we again see the grave cloths. But more than that, we see the face cloth, which is not with the other grave cloths, but over in another place by itself. In other words, we see round the inside of the tomb, but we do not see the body of Jesus!

At last, in scene 4, the Beloved Disciple himself enters the tomb. "And he saw, and he believed!" Believed what? The Evangelist first gives us time to reach our own conclusion. We are to put together the presence of the grave cloths and a missing body. We are to hear in the words "tomb," "take away the stone," and "face cloth" echoes of the story of Lazarus. And only after that does the Evangelist give us a clue or assure us that we are right: "You see, they did not yet [i.e., up to the time of these events] know the scripture that he must rise from the dead."

The first wave of discovery has spent itself. If there were no second wave, our raft would come to rest firmly on the shore of belief that Jesus had been raised from the dead. But the basis of our belief would be nothing more than the empty tomb and the empty grave cloths. It would not rest on personal encounter with the one come back from the dead.

But there is still enough water to keep us afloat. And so as it recedes, it carries us back (v. 11) to where the story began, before building up to a second wave that peaks and breaks in personal encounter.

The Second Wave

The receding water carries us back to Mary outside the tomb (scene 5). She is ignorant of all that Peter and the beloved disciple discovered. She is a woman in the depths of grief. She still assumes that some human being has removed the body. Would that she knew what we know! We eagerly await her discovery that Jesus has risen from the dead.

But even though we already know that the body of Jesus is gone while strangely the grave cloths have been left behind, the Evangelist has some surprises in store for us as well as for Mary. When she bends down to look into the tomb, she sees something we did not see before: two angels dressed in white, sitting at either end of the place where the body of Jesus should have been (scene 6). "Woman, why are you weeping?" they ask her. But Mary is so overwhelmed with loss and grief that she is entirely unimpressed by the presence of angels. All that matters is that "they took my Lord and I don't know where they put him."

Immediately after saying this, "she turned around and sees Jesus standing there" (scene 7). But never having known anyone to have come back from the dead, and blinded by grief, she fails to recognize Jesus; she takes him to be the gardener!

Mary's failure to recognize Jesus has often led to a discussion about whether Jesus' body was somehow changed to make it unrecognizable. The Evangelist nowhere hints that Jesus looked different. Perhaps the solution to the riddle lies elsewhere. Time and again we fail to recognize someone because we do not expect to see that person in a particular place.

A few years ago I was asked to lead a workshop in biblical storytelling for some pastors in North Carolina. At the beginning of the first session, I started to introduce the participants to the workshop agenda. I had barely begun when one of the men in the back row raised his hand and said, "Can I tell a story about you?" What was I to do? I said, "Okay," hoping that it would be appropriate. "When you were a little boy," he began, "I lived at your house for the summer. I was in charge of the morning playground. One day I sent you home for misbehaving. I was afraid your mother and dad were going to kick me out of the house." And immediately I burst out, "Nevin Feather!" I hadn't seen him in thirty years. And when I suddenly recognized him now, I had no doubt who he was. Although he was older, he did not look all that different to me. I had been looking right at him from the time he raised his hand and asked for permission to speak. But because I never expected to see him there, I did not recognize him. But his words about my boyhood and the summer playground had the same effect on me as Jesus' word "Mary" had on her. And I responded with joyful recognition.

"Rabboni!" Mary joyfully cries when Jesus speaks her name (scene 8). Perhaps she throws her arms around him, as I threw mine around my wife, Jane, when I returned from three weeks travelling by myself in Greece. Although the King James Version translates Jesus' next word to Mary as, "Touch me not" (scene 9), many modern translations say, "Do not hold onto me" or "Do not cling to me." Matthew tells us that the women took hold of Jesus' feet (Matt. 28:9). Jesus' command to Mary in John 20:17 may be a response to a similar action.

Jesus' next words to Mary are "for I have not yet ascended to the

Father." Some people have put this together with "Touch me not,"
and taken the combination to mean that there was something odd
about Jesus' body because he had not yet ascended. But the
meaning of Jesus' words may be quite different. Maybe it's the
physical contact that must be severed. Remember that an important concern of Jesus during his conversation with the disciples at
their last meal together (John 13-17) is his need to return to the
Father and their desire to have him stay with them. It may be that
with her joyful shout, "Rabboni!" Mary throws her arms around
Jesus, ecstatic at physically possessing once more the one she had
lost. By telling her "Don't hold on to me," Jesus is telling her that,
though he is risen, physical contact is not to be hers or the disciples' again. He has risen from the dead, but as he told his
disciples at the table, his physical presence must depart from them
to the Father, so that he can send them the Spirit, who will em-
power them in a way they had not known before (John 14:12-17).

The Living Presence of Jesus

With Mary's cry of recognition, "Rabboni!" a long sequence of
discoveries has reached its climax in personal encounter with the
risen Jesus. But what is the purpose of telling this story in such a
highly dramatic fashion? Clearly not to chronicle the details of the
event so that we may know exactly what happened. It is to involve
us in the experience of the event. John's account of the discovery
of the empty tomb differs significantly from that of the other three
Evangelists. Most of the differences have the effect of drawing us
into the drama. The tantalizing suspense created by the long and
gradual sequence of discovery, the vividness and sympathetic
portrayal of the characters' feelings and actions, the anticipation of
discovery generated by the discrepancy between the information
John gives us in verse 9 and Mary's ignorance of it (vv. 11-15)—all
these things serve to catch us up in the events of the story.

But why does John seek to involve us in the events? One
obvious purpose for telling dramatic stories is entertainment.
Another, however, is to teach, not just the mind but the heart. All
of John's stories we have considered so far in this resource book
clearly seek to educate the heart. John strives to arouse in us a love

of the woman of Samaria and the courage of the man who was
born blind. He seeks to address the disappointment we share with
Mary and Martha and to inspire us with the example of Jesus in
our own struggle for justice and truth.

But there is another purpose to John's stories—and indeed to the
stories of all the Evangelists—and it comes into clear focus in this
story of Jesus' resurrection: Stories of Jesus help to bring us into
the presence of the *living Jesus*. For most Christians throughout
history, Jesus has been far more than a person who actually lived
on earth in a particular historical time and place, a man who taught
us about loving both God and neighbor and about an eternal life
beyond death. The heartbeat of Christian faith is the belief that the
human being who taught us these things is also a living presence
among us, empowering us to live here and now the life to come.
The sole purpose of the story of Mary Magdalene, of Peter and the
beloved disciple, and of their discovery that Jesus had risen from
the dead, is to lead us to an encounter with the living Jesus.
Through that encounter we hear his assurance that he has returned
to the Father so that he can send us the Spirit. The other stories
considered so far teach us about love for enemies and courage when
we are threatened by them, and about God's care for us in grief and
God's power to create in us a life that will never die. John 20:1-18
teaches us that the Jesus we meet in the Gospel stories is alive
among us today, empowering us to live as he has taught us.

*About fifteen years ago on the island of Crete I had a conversation
with a Greek Orthodox monk named Fr. Palamos. We were talking
about Jesus, and he was saying things about Jesus that I knew were
nowhere recorded in the Gospels. Greatly distressed I said to him, "How
can you say that? There is nothing like that at all in the New Testament!" "What do I care about the New Testament?" he shot back. "I
know Jesus because he is here!"*

*I was flabbergasted by the priest's disregard for the evidence of the
Gospels, which I had been studying in detail for years. My intense
interest was in the questions, What did Jesus really say? Did he say
everything the Evangelists attribute to him? I had even questioned the
authenticity of everything that was recorded in the Gospels about Jesus.
How then could I believe things that were not recorded about him at all?*

*But as that conversation came back to me many times in the months
that followed, I realized that Fr. Palamos had opened to me something*

central to the Christian faith that I had missed. A vital Christian life did not feed off the inspired and inspiring teachings of a dead teacher. Christians who live the faith are constantly being nourished by Jesus' living spirit.

How, I wondered, could Jesus become a living reality for me? As I pondered this question, I realized that I had already begun to live the answer in the years since graduate school, while I was learning to tell the stories of Jesus aloud. The real tempo and emotion of the stories had been taught me by my fellow graduate student Tom Boomershine. Also, the clearest sense I had ever had of Jesus' presence had come years before my trip to Crete, while I was learning Mark's story of Jesus in Gethsemane and was trying to find the most fitting emotions with which to tell it. As I told it to myself and tried to recreate in sound Jesus' feelings of distress and grief, I began to feel that Jesus was there with me, sharing my own fear about my own inevitable death.

The foundation of the Christian faith is the belief that the sense of Christ's presence I felt while telling myself that story of Jesus is a very real presence, the presence of a person who has risen from the dead. Many people today will readily dismiss as false the Christian claim that the presence of Jesus experienced through story is a real presence. They will call it an illusion, a figment of the imagination. We cannot prove that they are wrong, of course. But we can make a good case for the imagination as a doorway, not only into illusion, but into hitherto undiscovered reality as well. When I am caught up in a powerful story about a person whose race, sex, age, class, culture, or religion is different from my own, my imagination puts me in touch with an experience that is very real but not accessible to me firsthand. The history of science is also full of stories of people who imagined a world that was very different from the world everyone around them saw or thought they saw. Copernicus, for example, imagined that, contrary to what was "obvious" to everyone, the earth revolved about the sun, not the sun about the earth. The modern study called the sociology of knowledge makes it plain that *all* perceptions of reality are in fact in part acts of the imagination, even the view that the universe is a closed system of cause and effect, devoid of God or of any divine purpose.

We all live by faith in something, either by faith in the dominant worldview of our culture or by faith in some alternative view. The stories of the New Testament invite us to live by faith in a reality that the earliest followers of Jesus claim they experienced firsthand. A few discovered Jesus' tomb empty of his body. Many more saw him with the wounds of crucifixion on a body able to pass through a locked door. Even more have felt the power of his Spirit enabling them to live and act in ways hitherto impossible for them. These followers of Jesus told stories of their experiences. And it is through their stories that the reality they knew may be opened up to each of us.

Chapter Six

Failure and Forgiveness
Peter

Words underlined or set in bold and italic type are significant verbal threads that sew these stories together. They will be discussed in this chapter.

John 1:40-42

⁴⁰ One of the two who heard John speak and followed him [Jesus], was Andrew, Simon Peter's brother. ⁴¹ He first found his brother Simon and said to him, "We have found the Messiah" (which is translated Anointed). ⁴¹ He brought Simon to Jesus, who looked at him and said, "You are *Simon the son of John.* You are to be called Cephas" (which means [in Greek] Peter, [in English, Rock]).

John 13:36-38

³⁶ Simon Peter said to him, "Lord, where are you going?" Jesus answered, "Where I am going, you cannot **follow** me now; but you shall **follow** afterward."

³⁷ Peter said to him, "Lord, why can I not **follow** you now? I will lay down my life for you." ³⁸ Jesus answered, "Will you lay down your life for me? Very truly, I tell you, before the cock crows, till you have denied me three times."

John 18:15-27

¹⁵ Simon Peter **followed** Jesus, and so did another disciple. Since that disciple was known to the high priest, he went with Jesus into the courtyard of the high priest, ¹⁶ but Peter was standing outside at the gate. So the other disciple, who was known to the high

priest, went out, spoke to the woman who guarded the gate, and brought Peter in.

¹⁷ The woman said to Peter, "Surely you're not one of this man's disciples, too!" He said, "I am not!"

¹⁸ Now the slaves and the police had made a <u>charcoal fire</u> because it was cold, and they were standing around it and warming themselves. Peter also was standing with them and warming himself.

[Annas's Interrogation of Jesus, vv. 19-24]

²⁵ Now Simon Peter was standing and warming himself. They said to him, "Surely you're not one of this man's disciples, too!" He denied it and said, "I am not!"

²⁶ One of the slaves of the high priest, a relative of the man whose ear Peter had cut off, asked, "Did I not see you in the garden with him?" ²⁷ Again Peter denied it, and at that moment the cock crowed.

John 21:15-22
[Setting: the beach by the Sea of Tiberius (21:1), after a breakfast of fish and bread around a <u>charcoal fire</u> (21:9)]

¹⁵ When they had finished breakfast, Jesus said to Simon Peter, *"Simon, son of John,* do you love me more than these?" He said to him, "Yes, Lord; you know that I love you." Jesus said to him, "Feed my lambs."

¹⁶ A second time he said to him, *"Simon, son of John,* do you love me?" He said to him, "Yes, Lord; you know that I love you." Jesus said to him, "Tend my sheep."

¹⁷ He said to him the third time, *"Simon, son of John,* do you love me?" Peter felt grieved because he said to him the third time, "Do you love me?" And he said to him, "Lord, you know everything; you know that I love you." Jesus said to him, "Feed my sheep."

¹⁸ Very truly, I tell you, when you were younger, you used to fasten your own belt and to go wherever you wished. But when you grow old, you will stretch out your hands, and someone else will fasten a belt around you and take you where you do not wish to go." ¹⁹ (He said this to indicate the kind of death by which he would glorify God.) After this he said to him, "**Follow** me."

²⁰ Peter turned and saw following them the disciple whom Jesus

loved; he was the one who had reclined next to Jesus at the supper and had said, "Lord, who is it that is going to betray you?" [21] When Peter saw him, he said to Jesus, "Lord, what about him?" [22] Jesus said to him, "If it is my will that he remain until I come, what is that to you? You **follow** me!"

Jesus in Pain

Bill was in his 50s. He had come to Lancaster Seminary after a long business career during which he also served as a lay leader in his church. We were in my office, and I was teaching him the story in John 21:15-17, of Jesus and Peter talking on the beach after Jesus' resurrection.

Bill got the words of the story down very quickly. So we began to explore the feelings of the story. I asked Bill, "How do you think Peter must have felt when he replied to Jesus' question?" Bill was well-acquainted with the larger story of Peter's relationship with Jesus. "After denying Jesus, Peter must have felt very ashamed of himself," he said.

Next we turned to the question of our own experiences. I asked Bill if he could recall a time in his life when he let someone down the way Peter had let Jesus down. But Bill didn't go along with my question. Instead, he began to tell me about his relationship with his father. His father had abandoned his family when Bill was a teenager. Some years later Bill was walking along a city street in Florida when he saw his father coming towards him. He stopped and waited. His father walked right up to him. Bill said, "Dad!" His father looked at him curiously for a moment and then continued his walk down the street without saying a word.

Bill felt devastated. "I know just how Jesus must have felt when he sat with Peter there on the beach and asked him, 'Do you love me?' He felt deep, crushing pain."

Bill's story opened up an entirely new dimension of this Bible story to me. For some time I had been saying to my class on the Gospel of John that if I had been Jesus there on the beach, I would have been very cold and distant towards Peter. Jesus' use of Peter's formal name, "Simon, son of John," suggests that this is how Jesus felt, too. Whenever my mother got really provoked with me when I was a child, she would let loose with my full and formal name!

Bill's experience suggested a feeling I had not even thought of: Jesus overwhelmed with pain, the pain of having been abandoned by one of his closest friends. In the course of learning and exploring and sharing the stories with another person, I had something new revealed to me about Jesus. When I fail him, I break his heart and fill him with deep loneliness at being let down by one who professes to love him. The story of my relationship with Jesus had begun a new chapter. Through Bill Jesus had made known to me a new dimension of himself and how he feels about me.

The conversation between Jesus and Peter, the concluding conversation of John's Gospel, begins as the story of two friends in pain. How did this situation come about? The story is familiar enough.

According to John 18:15-27, while Jesus was being interrogated by Annas, the high priest, about his teaching and his disciples, Peter stood by a charcoal fire warming himself. There he denied that he was one of Jesus' disciples. Now, on the shore of the Sea of Tiberius, Jesus makes another charcoal fire and there confronts Peter with what he did.

But the story actually begins even before Peter's denial. It starts in John 13:36-38, around the supper table during Jesus' last meal with his disciples. There Peter asks Jesus, "Lord, where are you going?" Jesus replies that he is about to go where Peter is not yet prepared to follow; he will follow later. But Peter cannot imagine being unable to follow Jesus immediately, no matter where Jesus might be going. He is willing even to die for Jesus! In reply Jesus tells him that Peter does not yet have what it takes to do that; on the contrary, he will repeatedly deny any association with Jesus.

At the end of the story of Peter's three denials, John says nothing about whether Peter realized what he had just done. Matthew, Mark, and Luke all report that Peter left the house of the high priest and wept. John omits any report of Peter's grief and develops the incident into an unforgettable dialogue between Jesus and Peter in the face-to-face encounter after Jesus' resurrection.

Unfinished Business

Simon, son of John, do you love me more than these? These are Jesus' opening words to Peter there on the beach around that charcoal fire (John 21:15). It was their first conversation since Peter denied he was one of Jesus' own. Scripture readers usually deliver these words with the detached feeling of a psychiatrist gathering some basic information from a client, or perhaps with mild disappointment and sadness. But think. How would you have felt if you had been Jesus? Recall how Bill felt when his father passed him by. Has anyone ever broken a promise to you? Has a person who claimed to be your friend ever betrayed your friendship? If I had been Jesus, I would have been filled not with mild disappointment but with deep disappointment, and my disappointment would have been mixed with personal pain and with not a little anger. Would Jesus have been invulnerable to a personal rebuff, or like me could he be hurt by someone who claims to love him? Would he have been warmly understanding and immediately forgiving, or would he have been upset at Peter's denial?

Many people see the Jesus of John's Gospel as divine power wearing a body but as a person completely in control of all that takes place and emotionally unaffected by what people do. It is true that in John's Gospel Jesus acts primarily at the prompting of God rather than in compassionate response to human distress. Remember his tardy response to the urgent summons to come heal Lazarus (John 11:1-6). It is also true that John emphasizes Jesus' awareness of and control over the things that happen to him. He lays down his life of his own choosing; no one takes it from him (10:18). He foresees Peter's denials (13:38).

But over the course of John's long story, Jesus is intensely moved in response to events and the people he is close to. He loves people (11:5; 13:1). He is deeply shaken or angry in response to the death of Lazarus (11:33, 38). He is greatly distressed in the face of his imminent betrayal (13:21). He rejoices (11:15; 15:11; 17:13). He weeps (11:35). He chides Nicodemus (3:10); he is distressed at the request of the royal official (4:48); he becomes impatient with Philip (14:8-9).

Many Christians cannot conceive of Jesus as angry and grieved by the way other people treat him. They strip Jesus of those emotions when they read stories about him in the Bible. Maybe they do so because the Bible seldom tells how Jesus felt when he spoke. But a detached Jesus, a man unaffected by how people behave toward him, is not the Jesus depicted in the Gospel of John.

Although the references to Jesus' feelings toward other people are few, they suggest that John intended the words of Jesus to be filled with depth and richness. We can read them in this way.

When the Word became flesh in the voice and gesture of the Fourth Evangelist, that creative Word, through whom all things came into being and without whom not anything was made that was made, became heart as well as mind, feeling as well as knowledge. And indeed Jesus' words to Peter in John 21:15 cry out in pain and anger.

Simon, son of John. Why does Jesus call Peter by this name? When Jesus had first met Peter, he said to him, "You are Simon the son of John. You are to be called Cephas," which to Greek-speaking listeners means Peter, to English-speaking listeners, Rock. Why now, at the end of the Gospel, does Jesus not call this man Cephas, the new name he gave him when they met? Because, standing before that other charcoal fire in the courtyard of the high priest, this man named Rock had failed to be a rock! His loyalty to Jesus had crumbled each time someone there observed that he was a follower of Jesus. For good reason Jesus calls him by a name that has nothing to do with their close relationship: Simon, son of John. It is Peter's turn to be treated like a stranger, just as in the court of the high priest he treated Jesus like a stranger! Think for a moment. How might Jesus have spoken that name, Simon, son of John ? With what feelings might he have addressed Peter?

I once was pastor of a church that had just been through a period of conflict. A significant percentage of the members had left the church because of it. When I visited one man and listened to his story of the trouble, he told me about an ugly meeting where he walked out. During this meeting, he reported, people who had known each other by their first names and nicknames all their lives began to address each other as Mr. So-and-So and Mrs. So-and-So. They resorted, that is, to formal names more appropriate to the anger they felt toward one another. They distanced themselves from one another.

I think that if I had been Jesus addressing Peter there on that beach, I would have spoken his name with at least a bit of anger. "But Jesus knew Peter was going to deny him!" you may protest. Jesus' knowledge of what Peter would do does not disqualify Jesus from being angry with Peter. My wife, Jane, knows me very well and is good at predicting some of my behavior. That does not prevent her from occasionally bursting out in anger, "I *knew* you were going to do that!" Centuries before Jane or Jesus, Jonah fumed at God when God saw the repentant Ninevites and relented from destroying them. "I *knew* that you are a gracious God and merciful, slow to anger, and abounding in steadfast love, and ready to relent from punishing," exploded Jonah. And the storyteller tells us that to Jonah God's mercy was "very displeasing" and Jonah was "angry" (Jonah 4:1-4).

Do you love me more than these? Jesus asks Peter concerning his love. Love is more than a special way of feeling; it is also a special way of behaving. In fact, according to Jesus its highest expression is in doing precisely what Peter at the supper table vowed to do for Jesus: lay down his life for his friend (13:37; 15:13). Jesus, too, made that highest expression of love the goal of his sojourn on earth. Jesus made love the sum of his command to his disciples: by loving one another all people will know that the disciples are his (13:35).

Is it conceivable that Jesus spoke with cool detachment when he inquired about something so important to him as love? Can Jesus have been emotionally uninvolved in and unaffected by the failure of his most outwardly enthusiastic disciple to do what he commanded?

More than these. These words obviously mean "do you love me more than these other disciples love me." Peter's vow at the supper table set his love for Jesus apart from the love of the other disciples (13:36-37). Peter's vow to lay down his life for Jesus, a promise he failed to keep, makes Peter fully and shamefully aware of just what Jesus meant.

Yes, Lord; you know that I love you. It is not until the third time Jesus asks Peter if he loves him that John tells us explicitly how Peter felt: "Peter felt grieved" (John 21:17). Nevertheless, it is likely that when the Evangelist told or read the story, he portrayed Peter from the very beginning as a man broken and steeped in shame. The episodes concerning Peter that build up to Jesus' question in verse 15 (13:36-38; 18:15-27) all point to this conclusion. So does John's portrayal of Peter throughout his Gospel as a character who is very sensitive and responsive to Jesus (6:68; 13:6-11; 20:3ff; 21:7, 11).

The Evangelist's larger story of Peter also suggests that the Living Bible and the Phillips' translations are wrong in distinguishing between the two Greek words for love here, *agapao* and *phileo*. The result of this distinction is to present Peter as one who does not know what Jesus is talking about. Jesus asks him, "Do you love [*agapao*] me?" Does Peter answer, "Yes, Lord, you know I'm your friend [*phileo*]"? This is a very unlikely interpretation of the conversation. Throughout his Gospel, and in this short conversation in particular, John exhibits a fondness for synonyms (feed/ tend, lambs/sheep, two different Greek words for "you know"). It seems that as a storyteller he simply likes to vary his expression.

If there is any significance in John's use of two different Greek words for love here, it is probably to be explained by John 15:13. There he defines what it means to be a friend [*philos*] precisely in terms of a love [*agape*] that leads one to do what Peter promised but failed to do: lay down his life for his friend.

Feed my lambs. All the notes John has struck in this conversation so far—the setting of the charcoal fire, Jesus' use of Peter's formal name, Jesus' question concerning Peter's superior love—echo Peter's promise to lay down his life for Jesus and resound with his shame and failure to do so. Jesus' command, "Feed my lambs," is one more such note.

The echoes may not be clear to listeners at first. Neither the word feed (Greek *boske*) nor the word lambs (Greek *arnia*) have been sounded in John's Gospel so far. But when Jesus repeats this command with the words "tend" (*poimaine*) and "sheep" (*probata*)" (v. 16), those words clearly reverberate with Jesus' words in John 10:1-18: the Good Shepherd (*poimen*) lays down his life for the sheep (*probaton*). Jesus' command, "Feed my lambs," is a command to engage in the work of caring for the sheep (in 21:15). This means not only leading the sheep out to pasture (10:3, 9) but defending them against wolves, possibly at the price of the shepherd's own life (vs. 11, 15).

At the supper table Peter promised, as a good shepherd would, to lay down his life for Jesus. In the courtyard of the high priest, Peter acted like a hireling, who "sees the wolf coming and leaves the sheep and runs away" (10:12). What Peter was not able to do for Jesus in the high priest's courtyard, Jesus commands him to do now for the sheep. Indeed, after Jesus finishes grilling Peter about his failure to love him the way a friend should love (21:15-17), he prophesies that Peter will die as Jesus himself died (vv. 18-19).

A second time he said to him . . . (v. 16). He said to him the third time . . . (v. 17). Why does Jesus ask Peter the same question again and again?

When I was a teenager, my younger brother, Ed, and I were in the living room having an argument. He was sitting slouched down in an armchair with the ankle of one leg perched on the knee of the other. I was so mad at him that I walked over, took hold of the foot that was stuck up in the air, and gave it a wrenching twist. My mother was not pleased. She sent me to my room. After several hours, she made her way up the stairs and sat down on the edge of my bed where I was lying.

"Are you sorry for what you did to Edwin?" she asked.

"Yeh, I'm sorry," I replied.

"Are you really sorry?" she asked again.

"Yeh, I said I'm sorry," I answered once more.

The question came yet a third time. "Are you sorry enough that you can come down and behave yourself?" And with added vehemence I declared my change of heart once more.

This was my mother's way of making her point, and she employed it on more occasions than this one. A single vow of contrition was not enough to assure her that I had considered the seriousness of what I had done. Repetition was required.

This experience returns to my memory whenever I hear Peter's interrogation by Jesus. It is not that Peter had denied Jesus three times, so Jesus quizzes Peter three times. It is rather that saying something three times often yields a sense of completeness and satisfaction. For that reason people often do or say things in threes. Remember, for example, some of Jesus' parables: three different servants are entrusted with the master's money (Matt. 25:14-30); a priest, a levite, and a Samaritan come near the man lying along the road (Luke 10:30-35).

But Jesus' thrice repeated question to Peter does more than make sure Peter will think deeply enough about his denials. It also confronts Peter with the grief and pain he inflicted on Jesus. It brings Peter to the point of tasting Jesus' suffering himself and provides the occasion for Jesus to express his own pain and anger. We see that Jesus, too, has feelings. He needs to be heard by this man for whom he cares so deeply.

When we hear this story or read it aloud, the feelings expressed by both Peter and Jesus are critical to its meaning. Will we read Peter's words in such a way that we show him to be insensitive and morally shallow, a person who has no idea what a terrible thing he has done to Jesus? Or will we infuse his words with the shame we feel when we fail to keep our promise to someone we dearly love? Will we find in Peter a companion who, before our time, knew the deep humiliation of failure? Can Peter bring our shame into the presence of Jesus?

How will Jesus respond to us when Peter brings us into Jesus' presence? If we come to him in shame, will he brush our feelings aside? Will he dismiss them with a wave of the hand as unimportant? Will Jesus be warmly understanding and immediately forgiving of anything we may have done? Or will he be hurt by our treatment of others, sharing their feelings of pain and anger? Will Jesus be as deeply crushed as the others have been? Will the way to forgiveness be cheap and painless for us, or will Jesus drive us over the agonizing road of the truth of what we have done?

After Peter's third vow of love for Jesus and Jesus' third command to "Feed my sheep," Jesus is satisfied with Peter's response and ready to move on. Peter himself has now experienced the grief and humiliation of being treated like a stranger; Jesus has shared his own pain and anger. The time has come to put Peter's shameful deed behind them. Having once prophesied Peter's failure to fill his promise (13:38), Jesus now goes on to prophesy his success.

When you were younger. The sentence that begins with these words paints a pair of pictures. On the one hand, there is a young man whose hands are limber as he ties his own belt about his waist and sets off on his merry way. On the other, there is an old man with hands crippled with arthritis, who is unable any longer even to tie a knot. He is dependent on others to care for him and, therefore, has no choice but to go where they decide.

John follows this prophetic metaphor of Jesus, so typical of the way the prophets speak in the Bible, with an explanation. The picture has a double meaning: Jesus said this "to indicate the kind of death by which he would glorify God." These words echo earlier words about Jesus' own death. In John 12:33, Jesus spoke of being *lifted up* from the earth, and the Evangelist explained that he said this "to indicate the kind of death he was to die." In John 18:32, the Jewish leaders demand from Pilate *a Roman execution*, and John explained that this was "to indicate the kind of death he was to die." Now Jesus speaks of Peter's *outstretched hands*, and again the Evangelist explains that this was "to indicate the kind of death by which he would glorify God." The words "lifted up" and the demand for a Roman execution show that Jesus' manner of death will be crucifixion. Peter's outstretched hands show that in following Jesus by laying down his life for Jesus, Peter will also die by crucifixion.

Follow me! John concludes the conversation between Peter and Jesus by returning from John's own explanation of the meaning of Jesus' prophecy to Jesus' final words to Peter: "Follow me." The command reverberates with echoes of the conversation at the supper table (13:36–38). Follow me as you promised. Follow me to where you were not able to follow before. Lay down your life for me. Follow me to death. Peter will have a second chance.

I remember visiting a family in the waiting room of a hospital. Eight years before they had brought their baby girl to church and promised God to do all they could to lead her toward an understanding of the Christian gospel and into the service of Jesus Christ. They hadn't been to church or Sunday School since that day. She now lay in a room nearby, wired to a dozen machines. The child had run out onto the highway in front of their house and been hit by a truck. "If only God will let her live," they cried out in anguish, "we'll start bringing her to church!" God answered their prayer. Their little girl recovered completely. And so they brought her to church—for two Sundays.

The urgency of need summons forth from us passionate vows of dedication. But once the need is satisfied, ardor cools, and second thoughts have room to play. That is what happened with this mother and father. It also happened with Peter.

Back in Jesus' good graces, the pain of separation relieved, Peter turns around and sees the disciple whom Jesus loved following. "Lord, what about him?" he stammers, overtaken by the full weight of Jesus' assurance that he, Peter, would indeed keep his earlier passionate but thoughtless promise to lay down his life for Jesus. Peter's need for forgiveness satisfied, he suddenly wonders whether he hasn't been a bit excessive with his promise. Are others going to get away with less than he will? Does he really want to love Jesus more than the others love him?

I cannot help but laugh at Peter here. But I laugh because he is so much like me. Perhaps, since Jesus finally did build the church on wobbly rocks like Peter, since he finally did care for his flock with the help of shepherds who waver between being good shepherds and hirelings—perhaps there is hope for me as a follower of Jesus!

And how does Jesus respond to Peter's flirtation with going back on the promise? "If it is my will that he remain until I come, what is that to you?" Does Jesus burst out in anger? Does he slap his hand to his forehead, laughing and crying at the same time in exasperation? I can just see him start to tear his hair out over this impossible disciple, and Peter sheepishly mumbling an apology, his face red as a beet. Then Jesus points his finger at Peter and says, "*You* follow me!"

The Rock of Our Faith

The Gospel story itself ends on this note. The Evangelist still has a few closing comments to make. But Jesus' encounters with the Samaritan woman, the blind man, Mary, Martha, Lazarus, Pilate, Mary Magdalene, and Peter are at an end. What is the impact of these stories?

The stories of these encounters confront us with a living person. He lived almost two thousand years ago. But as Christians we believe that he rose from death and is alive and with us today. The stories of his encounters with people of old mediate to us experiences of his presence, addressing our own lives in many ways.

These stories call us to a relationship. That is primary. They do not call us to a certain way of thinking or to a particular pattern of behavior—at least not at first. They call us into a relationship from which our speech and action flows. And that relationship is with the Creator of all life who became flesh in Jesus Christ, made manifest the divine vulnerability to a beloved creation, triumphed over our rebellion and failure, and is now present in the Spirit challenging and empowering us to truly live.

The story of the encounter between Jesus and Peter is a good note on which to end the Gospel. The Evangelist's purpose in telling it was "so that you may come to believe that Jesus is the Messiah, the Son of God, and that through believing you may have life in his name [20:31]."

But fear and resentment trip us up as we seek to make our way along the path of that life. We fall. But Jesus picks us up and gives us another chance. Peter in particular shows how, when we stumble and fall, we inflict pain on God. The God who meets us in Jesus Christ is not unaffected by our promises and our failures. God loves us, and is made glad by our love, and is overcome with anguish at our disloyalty. God does not take our failures lightly or dismiss them. God calls us to account, often by confronting us with the pain we have inflicted on God and by giving us a taste of that pain ourselves. John's story of Peter, read or told as I have suggested, can renew this revelatory experience time and again as we commit ourselves to Jesus and then fall back, commit ourselves again and fall back again. It calls us to dare great things for God despite the courage that we lack. It is a story filled with hope.

Notes

Chapter 1—Prejudice and Oneness in Christ

1. See Joachim Jeremias, *Jerusalem in the Time of Jesus* (Philadelphia: Fortress Press, 1969), 352-54, for an account of the changing relationships.

2. If I were writing for a general audience, out of respect for persons who are not Christians, I would use C.E., meaning "Common Era," in place of A.D. "Anno Domini," "in the year of our Lord." Since I am writing for Christian readers, I retain A.D. as an expression of how our faith shapes our reading of human history.

3. Louis H. Feldman, trans., *Josephus*, vol. 9 (Cambridge: Harvard Univ. Press, 1965), 24-27. Used by permission.

4. Jeremias, *Jerusalem in the Time of Jesus*, 353.

5. Raymond E. Brown quoting Lagrange in *The Gospel According to John. The Anchor Bible*, vol. 29 (Garden City: Doubleday, 1966), 175.

6. Amos Wilder, *The Language of the Gospel* (New York: Harper & Row, 1964), 64.

7. *Aboth*, 1,5. See Jeremias, *Jerusalem in the Time of Jesus*, 359-60.

8. *Niddah* 4,1. *The Mishnah*, Herbert Danby, trans. (London: Oxford Univ. Press, 1933), 748.

9. For a very informative and stimulating discussion of Jesus' speaking of God as Father, see Brian Wren, *What Language Shall I Borrow? God-Talk in Worship: A Male Response to Feminist Theology* (New York: Crossroad, 1990), 183-88.

Chapter 2—The Gift and Cost of Sight

1. Tom Boomershine (see Preface).

Chapter 3—Disappointment and Fulfillment

1. George R. Beasley-Murray, *John*, Word Biblical Commentary, vol. 36 (Waco: Word Books, 1987), 188.

2. Ibid., 192-93.

Chapter 4—The Struggle for Justice

1. Feldman, *Josephus*, 9:43-47.

2. *Harper's Bible Dictionary*, s.v. "Messiah."

3. Gerald Sloyan, *John*, Interpretation: A Bible Commentary for Teaching and Preaching (Atlanta: John Knox, 1988), 199.

4. F. C. Conybeare, trans., *Philostratus, the Life of Apollonius of Tyana*, vol. 1 (Cambridge: Harvard Univ. Press, 1912), 59. Used by permission.

Chapter 5—Grief Turned to Joy

1. Translation from C. K. Barrett, *The New Testament Background* (London: SPCK, 1961), 15. Used by permission.

Bibliography

Barrett, C. K. *The New Testament Background*. New York: Harper & Row, 1961.

Beasley-Murray, George R. *John*. Word Biblical Commentary, vol. 36. Waco: Word Books, 1987.

Brown, Raymond E. *The Gospel According to John (i–xii)*. The Anchor Bible, vol. 29. Garden City: Doubleday, 1966.

Conybeare, F. C., trans. *Philostratus, the Life of Apollonius of Tyana*, vol. 1. Cambridge: Harvard Univ. Press, 1912.

Danby, Herbert, trans. *The Mishnah*. London: Oxford Univ. Press, 1933.

Feldman, Louis H., trans. *Josephus*, vol. 9. Cambridge: Harvard Univ. Press, 1965.

Harper's Bible Dictionary. Paul J. Achtemeier, ed. San Francisco: Harper & Row, 1985.

Jeremias, Joachim. *Jerusalem in the Time of Jesus*. Philadelphia: Fortress Press, 1969.

Sloyan, Gerald. *John*. Interpretation: A Bible Commentary for Teaching and Preaching. Atlanta: John Knox, 1988.

Wilder, Amos. *The Language of the Gospel*. New York: Harper & Row, 1964.

Wren, Brian. *What Language Shall I Borrow? God-Talk in Worship: A Male Response to Feminist Theology*. New York: Crossroad, 1990.

Pass It On

Telling and Hearing Stories from John

Leader's Guide

Gilbert L. Bartholomew

A Kaleidoscope Series Resource

United Church Press
Cleveland, Ohio

Objectives of the Course

Each person who completes this course will be able to—
1. Read six stories from John's Gospel in a life-like way and tell several, whole or in part, from memory.
2. Identify personal stories of experiences, relationship, conversations, and events that connect with John's stories.
3. Develop creative responses to the stories.

Learning and Leadership Style

This manual makes the following assumptions about leadership and learning style:

· The book for this course is for adults. But all the activities in the Leader's Guide can be done with participants of every age, beginning with elementary school children.

· People of all ages share stories of their experiences daily. When they do so, they strive to communicate to others not only what happened but how the experience felt. With practice we can all learn to tell and read Bible stories for the same purpose.

· People of all ages have a wealth of experience recorded in their memories that connect with stories in the Bible. When someone primes the pump, the connecting stories start to rise to the surface.

· Learning a story from the Bible by heart does not mean memorizing it word for word, but rather event by event. Three good rules for memorization are these: (1) Keep the events in order. (2) Don't add things, such as how a character felt or why a character said something, but also don't omit important elements of the story. (3) Quote the actual words of the characters as though you were that character speaking.

· Some people, especially children, learn to tell a story by heart very quickly; others have to struggle to remember even a little. We can all learn a story by heart if we are willing to try, if we are given a simple method of remembering it that fits our own way of learning, and if we practice.

· How much of a Bible story a person learns by heart is immaterial. Even the effort to remember is a way of getting better acquainted with the story. Any part of the story a person learns may color the person's experience when carried in the memory through the day.

· Although some people may seem to be more creative than

others, what counts in this course is *doing what is suggested,* not the results of that action.

· Participants will have a wide range of abilities in relation to the "Suggested Components" of the course. You as the leader should encourage participants to give whatever they have to the group. *Involvement, not perfection, is the goal.*

· While the sessions are independent of one another in content, a progression from easy to more difficult in story reading and storytelling skills unfolds. All of the skills in the course, however, have been used with beginners in storytelling workshops. Newcomers can join the course at any time, so long as they are willing to give the storytelling suggestions a good try.

Time, Space, and Equipment

The course is designed for six two-hour sessions. A two-hour block of time is best because it allows for momentum to build as the group moves from one activity to the next. As the leader you will need to be alert to whether the group gets bogged down in a particular activity. If so, move the group on to the next one. A variety of experiences and involvement with each story is the chief goal. It is *not* necessary to use all the activities in each session.

If you must spread the activities of a session out over several time periods shorter than two hours, use a form of warm-up review at the beginning of the second or third segments on a given story. It is especially important for the initial session to be two hours in order to initate the group into the process to be used throughout the course.

The session plans in this Leader's Guide are designed for a group of fifteen to twenty people. But with a little adaptation, they can be used with any number of people, as all the activities are carried out either by the entire group or in teams of two. Sessions like those outlined in this guide have been conducted with hundreds of people in a large auditorium. Participants simply turned in their seats to face their partners. Sessions have also been conducted in an outdoor setting, where working pairs went for a walk by themselves to share the stories from the Bible and their personal stories.

Materials you will need include a chalkboard or newsprint. For a few activities each team of two will need a marker and a sheet of newsprint along with wall space and tape for hanging the sheet.

A VCR-VHS system is essential for showing the videotape that accompanies the course. The person who operates the system should review the tape before showing it, and it would be well for you to know the contents of the tape also.

Educational Components

Specific components are described under each session of this guide. Because more are suggested than can be used, you as leader will have to select ones to use, and you may want to introduce components of your own design. Here are the components used throughout the course:

1. The Book. This consists of six lesson chapters, one for each two-hour session. Adult participants will be encouraged to read the relevant chapter *after* each working session. In this way they will have an opportunity to *experience* the story *before they reflect* on it.

2. A videocassette. This accompanies the course and contains six segments, one for each of the six sessions.

Chapter 1: Prejudice and Oneness in Christ

Objectives

1. To establish an atmosphere of ease, openness, and partnership in the class learning process.

2. To state the objectives, outline, and learning style of the course and to clarify the expectations.

3. To share with the participants a vivid telling of John's story of the Samaritan woman whom Jesus met at the well.

4. To identify in words various emotions to be brought out in the telling of the story.

5. To share with another person one or more personal experiences that connect with the story.

Suggested Components

1. *Before Class.* You will be moving back and forth between working in pairs and sharing with the entire group. If you have a choice, arrange the chairs in a horseshoe to begin the course. This helps create the sense of a community that is open to receive more participants. Place the video equipment and the chalkboard or newsprint and easel in the opening of the horseshoe so that everyone can see it.

2. *Opening.* Begin the session with a hymn everybody knows from memory and loves to sing, such as "I Love to Tell the Story" or "Tell Me the Stories of Jesus." Then say Psalm 23 together.

3. *Introduction.* Have each participant find a partner. Give these directions: "Describe to the other the best storyteller you remember, or tell your partner your favorite Bible story." Note: If there is an odd number of participants, you as the leader should be the extra person's partner.

4. *Overview of the Course.* Reconvene the entire group. Inform the participants of the following: "In many courses we spend most of our time *talking about* the Bible. In this course we shall try to *get inside* the Bible and live it. We shall seek to experience six stories from the Gospel of John by speaking the words of the stories in true-to-life ways. We shall also lower our buckets into the deep well of our experiences in order to draw up stories of our own lives that connect with the events, the feelings, and the relationships in the biblical stories. And, finally, we shall seek to internalize the stories by committing parts of them to memory, so that they will be available to us through the day and the week for our personal meditation."

5. *The Story of the Samaritan Woman at the Well.*

a. Ask: "How many of you are familiar with the story of the Samaritan woman at the well (in the Gospel of John)? Without looking in our Bibles, let's see how much we can remember of the story as a group." Note: Solicit every detail anyone can remember. The order of the details does not matter. Some participants may remember details from other stories. That does not matter. Accept every contribution. The point is to stimulate their memories. If you as leader remember things no one mentions, offer clues to these to see if the participants can come up with the details themselves. For example, if no one mentions the disciples in the story, ask, "Who was Jesus with before he got to the well?" or "Who interrupted Jesus' conversation with the woman?"

b. Show Video Segment I. In this segment the author introduces the course and tells the story of the Samaritan woman in a dramatic way.

c. Discuss: "How is the video's dramatic way of sharing a Bible story similar to or different from your previous experience with Bible stories? Let's compare these especially in regard to the role of pauses and emotions." List the various emotions exhibited by the story-teller.

d. Focus on John 4:7b-26. Ask participants to get back with their partners and do the following: "Turn to the text of the story in the book. Read aloud scene 2 (vs. 7b-26)." One participant should read the words of Jesus and the other the words of the woman. They should be as dramatic as possible.

e. Give each team a chance to share with the entire group their favorite part.

f. In teams again suggest: "Try to recall your first personal encounter with a person of a different race, religion, or ethnic group. How old were you? Where were you? How did you feel? What did you say to each other? How has this experience helped shape your belief in Jesus as Savior of the world?"

6. *Suggestions for Going Further.*

a. Ask participants to jot down the directions you will give them, and state to the group the following: "The Bible stories we carry with us through the day help shape our lives. Each day this week set aside fifteen minutes to read aloud again all or part of John 4:7b-26. Also during that time reflect again on the connecting experiences you shared with your partner during the learning session. Try to recall yet more such stories. Close your prayer time with the verse about the living water from the hymn 'I Heard the Voice of Jesus Say.' During the day recall a favorite sentence or two from the Bible story and be alert for new connections occurring right under your nose!"

b. Tell the group: "Read chapter 1 of the book to enrich your understanding of the story and to personally appropriate the story. There the author describes the experiences of the characters and, from time to time, shares his own stories of connecting experiences. What stories of your own come to mind as you read chapter 1?"

7. *Closing.* Close with the hymn "I Heard the Voice of Jesus Say." Stanza 2 is about the living water Jesus gives.

Chapter 2: The Gift and Cost of Sight

Objectives

1. To share some personal experiences that connect with the Bible story of the man born blind.

2. To learn by heart scene 1 and one other scene of the story in John 9, as outlined in the book.

3. To participate in a telling of the entire story of the man born blind.

4. To help compose a verse of "Amazing Grace" based on a scene of the story.

Suggested Components

1. *Before Class.* Write on newsprint the verse to "Amazing Grace" in 5. below. Or compose your own verse that expresses the meaning of John 9:1-7 that could be sung to the hymn melody.

2. *Opening.*

a. Ask participants: "Share experiences you have had during the week while reading aloud and reflecting on the story of the Samaritan woman." Also: "As you read chapter 1, what stories of your own came to mind?" Note: Emphasize the *telling* of stories. Encourage participants to flesh out abstract observations.

b. Make the transition to this week's story by singing "Amazing Grace."

3. *The Story.*

a. Divide the group into teams of two in which each one tells the other stories of personal eye-opening experiences.

b. Reconvene the entire group in order to learn John 9:1-7.

Strategy: View Video Segment II, where the author teaches a small group of people John 9:1-7. First, he gives the group a line of the story, which they repeat. Next, everyone repeats the story in unison. Finally, each person tries to tell it alone. Ask your group members to join the video group in trying to learn the story.

Alternative strategy: Teach the group John 9:1-7 yourself, using the method on the videotape as your model.

c. List the remaining scenes of the story on newsprint or a chalkboard. Ask the group members to turn to the text of John 9 in the book. Have each team of two come forward to sign up for a scene of the story. Two or more teams may sign up for the same scene if all scenes are covered.

Give each team about 20 minutes during which time the partners will teach each other the scene of the story. Encourage them to try on each other the method demonstrated on Video Segment II.

d. Share the story. Tell the group: "We are now going to conduct an experiment. We are going to tell our way through the entire story of John 9:1-41. Each team will tell its scene of the story.

One member of your team should start. The other may help or take up the story in turn. You don't have to use the exact words. Just tell us what you remember." Note: It is very important that, as each team makes its contribution, you as leader praise each person for what he or she remembers. State to the group: "Some people have had more practice in memorizing than others but that each person's effort and contribution to the group is what counts. *Whatever you remember is something to take home with you.*"

4. *Reflection.* Ask each team to share with each other stories of experiences that connect with their part of the story. Here are some suggestions for connections to look for with each scene:

Scene 2. A time no one would believe you.

Scene 3. A time you, like the healed blind man, were questioned by someone in authority.

Scene 4. A time you, like the parents, didn't want to get involved in a conflict.

Scene 5. A time you, like the formerly blind man, challenged someone in authority.

Scene 6. A time your world fell apart, as the healed blind man's world fell apart.

Scene 7. A time you, like the Pharisees, were accused of an embarrassing error.

After 7 minutes, invite anyone who wishes to share her or his experience with the entire group to do so. Be prepared to share a story of your own if no one else has one.

5. *Creative Response.* Ask each team to compose a verse to "Amazing Grace" that tells their scene of the story. Emphasize that the purpose of this activity is not the product but active involvement with the story. Show the teams your own verse or the following example, which you may have written on a sheet of newsprint:

When Jesus came he made the clay
And he anointed me.
He said, "Go, wash in Siloam."
I washed, and now I see.

Students can write the words of their verses on a sheet of newsprint and hang it where everybody can see it. Then sing the verses together in the order of the scenes.

6. *Suggestions for Going Further.*

a. Say: "During your daily prayer time this week, tell yourself the story in John 9:1-7 or the later scene you learned by heart. Review the text in the book as necessary and meditate on the story by searching your memory for connecting experiences." Close with "Amazing Grace" or the verse you wrote for it.

b. Suggest: "Think about the various activities you have planned for the day ahead. Will there be an opportunity you will have to share John 9:1-7 with someone else? Will you be tucking your children into bed? Will you be leading devotions at a church meeting? Will you be visiting someone who is ill or grieving or lonely?"

c. End by stating, "Read chapter 2 for new ideas to ponder. Let the author's stories remind you to probe your memory for your stories."

7. *Closing.* Lead the class in singing their way through the story with the verses they composed.

Chapter 3: Disappointment and Fulfillment

Objectives

1. To share personal experiences that connect with the story of Mary and Martha.

2. To learn scene 5 of John 11 by heart.

3. To participate with gesture and movement alone (mime) in a telling of the entire story of Mary and Martha.

4. To make up a line to the hymn tune of "What Wondrous Love Is This?" in response to each scene of the story.

Suggested Components

1. *Opening.*

a. Share experiences participants had during the week with the story of the healing of the blind man. Ask: "As you read chapter 2, what stories of your own came to mind?"

b. Make the transition to this week's story in John 11 by singing "What Wondrous Love is This?" printed at the end of this leader's guide. The author sings it on Video Segment IIIa. You may wish to show that portion of the video and have the group sing along.

2. *The story.*

a. In groups of two have the class tell each other a personal experience of help arriving too late or of unanswered prayer.

b. Without looking in the Bible beforehand, work together as a group to remember everything you can about the story of Lazarus. Offer clues to parts of the story no one in the group mentions, but stop when the memories of the participants are exhausted. Don't continue with your own.

c. Learn John 11:38-44. Have group members pair up and turn to the text of the story of Lazarus in the book. Ask them to teach each other scene 5 of the story. Review Video Segment II for a model of the method. Give them about 15 minutes to learn the scene.

d. Call the group back together. Ask: "Who would be willing to start telling scene 5 of the story? You can tell as much as you remember, and then someone else can take over."

3. *Enlivening the Story.*

a. List the other scenes of the story on newsprint or a chalk-board. Combine scenes 6 and 7. Ask participants to read the entire story from the book and, in teams, to sign up for a scene on which they will focus. More than one team may sign up for the same scene, so long as all scenes are covered.

b. Explain: "Video Segment IIIb shows two people experimenting with different emotions in reading aloud scene 5 of the story of Lazarus. As the video team members try out different emotions in saying the words of the story, they share briefly experiences of their own when they felt similarly." Show this segment of the video.

c. Ask team members to use the video they just saw as a model for working on the scenes they have chosen.

4. *Creative Responses.*

a. Write on newsprint the following first part of the American folk hymn "What Wondrous Love Is This?"

What wondrous love is this, O my soul,
  O my soul,
What wondrous love is this, O my soul!
What wondrous love is this . . .

Hang it somewhere for all to see. Have each team finish the verse by making up lines that go with their story. They can write these on newsprint and hang them for all to see. Here is an example for scene 5:

> . . . That caused the Son of God
> To raise from death his friend as a sign,
>   as a sign,
> A sign of life for me without end.

b. Have the teams take ten minutes to work out a mime of their part of the story. In a mime a person tells the story without speaking, employing only action and gesture. The teams may do this in any way they desire. They may portray the actions or the feelings of the story. They may take different parts or act in unison. You as leader mime scene 5.

5. *Suggestions for Going Further.*

a. Suggest to the class, "Each day begin your time of prayer by miming your scene of the story or singing your verse of 'What Wondrous Love Is This?' "

b. Direct the group: "Then, recall the events of the past day. Did anything happen that connects with the story of Lazarus? Project the activities of the day ahead. Is anything coming up that connects with the story? Will there be any opportunity to share the story with someone else?"

c. Give this final suggestion: "During the course of the week, read chapter 3 in the book for enrichment. Read only part of the chapter each day. Pause to remember stories of your own experiences that connect with the story."

6. *Closing.* Mime the story by having a member of each team volunteer to enact his or her part of the story. Have the entire group respond to each mimed scene with the words of "What Wondrous Love Is This?" composed by the team for that scene. Begin with the traditional first verse; then proceed to mime scene 1.

Chapter 4: The Struggle for Justice

Objectives

1. To share personal experiences that connect with the story of Jesus and Pilate.

2. To observe the pattern of the story in John 18 and 19 created by the number of scenes and the changes of locale and characters.

3. To decide upon a word or image that captures the unique-ness of each scene of the story of Jesus and Pilate and the Jewish leaders and to use that word or image to remember that scene.

4. To decide which character in the story each participant identifies with most, and search the memory for experiences that may lead to that identification.

5. To try out different ways of saying the words of a given character, and to participate in a reading of the entire story.

Suggested Components

1. *Opening.*

a. Share experiences the class had during the week when reading the story of the raising of Lazarus. Ask the group: "As you read chapter 3, what stories of your own came to mind?"

b. Make the transition to this week's story of the Pilate trial in John 18 and 19 by singing "A Mighty Fortress Is Our God." Then, read aloud Isaiah 52:13–53:12.

2. *The Story.*

a. Divide the class into teams of two and tell each team to exchange a story of one of the following experiences:

· being caught in the middle of someone else's fight,

· being unjustly accused,

· standing up to someone bigger than you,

· telling the truth when it was risky,

· acting nonviolently.

b. Call the teams together and, without looking in the Bible, ask them to remember everything they can about the Pilate trial. Write what they recall on a chalkboard or newsprint chart.

c. On Video Segment IV, the author of the course tells John's story of Pilate. Show it. Ask the group to listen for all the things they listed during activity b.

d. Did group members hear anything they *did not* expect? If so, add it to the list you began. Did they miss anything they *did* expect? If so, direct their attention to the Pilate story in Matthew 27, Mark 15, and Luke 23. Ask them to explain their surprises in light of the other accounts.

e. Divide the group again into teams of two. Turn to the text of John's Pilate story in the book. Ask each team to observe the number of scenes and answer these three questions:

· Who are the characters in each scene?

· Where does the scene take place?

· What word or image distinctive to each scene might help you to remember what happens in it?

f. Reconvene the group and ask for a volunteer to tell the word or image picked for scene 1. Write it on newsprint or the chalkboard. Ask the two who picked that word or image to close the text and help each other tell that part of the story. Then do the same for the rest of the scenes.

3. *Reflection.* List "Pilate," "Jesus," and "Chief Priest" (standing for Jewish leaders in the story) on newsprint or a chalkboard. In teams ask the class to discuss this question, "Which of these characters can I identify with the best?" and to tell each other a story of a personal experience that leads them to make that identification.

4. *Enlivening the Story.* Assign each team responsibility for one of the three characters. Instruct the teams to go through the entire story, experimenting with different ways of saying the words of the character they selected. Try to connect each experiment with a personal story and to relate these stories during this part of the session.

5. *Suggestions for Going Further.* Use the model established for the preceding sessions.

6. *Closing.* Reconvene the group and ask for a volunteer to read the words of each character. You as leader read the words of the narrator and the soldiers. For the closing, read the story with different voices.

Chapter 5: Grief Turned to Joy

Objectives

1. To learn to tell John 20:1-18 from memory.

2. To share stories of personal experiences that connect with the story.

3. To have group members share with each other the meaning for them of Jesus' resurrection.

4. To compare John's story of the resurrection to the song, "In the Garden," whose author was inspired by the story.

5. To tell the John 20 story in mime.

Suggested Components:

1. *Opening.*

a. Elicit experiences the class had during the week with the story of Jesus' trial before Pilate. Ask: "As you read chapter 4, what stories of your own came to mind?"

b. Make the transition to this week's story by singing "In the Garden." This will be a song known by heart to some members of your group; it is in most Sunday school hymnals, but in few church hymnals that I have seen.

2. *The Story.*

a. Divide the group into teams of two. Then instruct them to share their personal stories of joyful reunion, of making an unusual discovery, or of not recognizing someone they knew.

b. Reconvene the group and recount together as much of the story of Mary Magdalene's encounter with Jesus as you can.

c. Turn to the text of John 20:1–18 in chapter 5 of the book. As a group, read the story aloud as dramatically as possible.

d. Ask the group to observe the number of acts and scenes in the story and to answer the following questions:

· Who are the characters in each scene?

· What word or image distinctive to each scene might help you to remember what happens in it?

Use the group's answers to construct an outline of the story on newsprint.

e. Show Video Segment V. In it two people are filling in the outline of the story created by the scene titles.

f. Divide the class again into teams. Ask the teams to fill in the outline of the story from memory, without looking at the text. Each team member should try it two or three times, reading the text aloud as necessary again after each try.

g. Reconvene the group and ask for a volunteer to tell the first scene of the resurrection story, another to tell the second, and so on. If the volunteer gets stuck, the team partner may assist.

3. *Reflection.* Ask the participants to find one or two others with whom they feel they could comfortably share their faith. Say to the group: "Christians interpret the resurrection of Jesus in different ways. Unfortunately, people who think one way often condemn those who think another way. Let this be a time of stimulating sharing on a central Christian belief. Here are some questions and

comments to help you get into this subject." (Write the following on newsprint or a chalkboard):

· What is the vital center of your Christian faith? Is the message of Jesus' resurrection part of it? In what way?

· People have experienced the presence of Jesus at various times: during private prayer, while listening to or reading a story of Jesus, during an event in which a group is trying to live out their Christian faith. Have you felt the presence of Jesus at any such time? Can you think of other instances?

4. *Creative Responses.*

a. Provide the group with the words to "In the Garden." Ask: "How many connections can you make between the song and the story. Where do you see differences between the two?" List them on newsprint or a chalkboard.

b. Divide the class into teams in order to mime the entire story, with each team doing a separate scene.

5. *Suggestions for Going Further.*

a. Use the model established in the preceding sessions.

b. Assign the reading of chapters 5 and 6 in the book for the next session.

6. *Closing.* Ask for two volunteers and two pinch-hitters to tell the two halves of the story. Ask for a volunteer to mime each half as the tellers narrate it.

Chapter 6: Failure and Forgiveness

Objectives

1. To share some personal experiences that connect with the story of Peter.

2. To learn by heart John 21:15-17, Peter's story.

3. To mime verses 18 through 19.

4. To experiment with various ways of saying verses 15 through 17 and to judge the appropriateness of each emotion in light of several other passages in the Gospel of John.

5. To develop a responsive reading by interspersing parts of the story with other passages from the Fourth Gospel.

6. To share experiences and ideas about using the stories in ministering to others.

Suggested Components

1. *Opening.*

a. Share experiences participants had during the week while reading the story of Jesus' resurrection from chapter 5. What stories of their own came to mind?

b. Make the transition to this week's story of Peter by singing "I Love to Tell the Story" from your church hymnal.

2. *The Story.*

a. Divide the group into teams of two. Then share stories of injuring or being injured by someone you love.

b. Reconvene as a group: Without using your Bibles, recall together as much as you can of the story in which Jesus asks Peter "Do you love me?" and then commands Peter to feed his sheep.

c. Teach the group John 21:15-17, using the method modeled on Video Segment II.

d. In teams of two develop a mime of verses 18 and 19. Invite the teams to share their mimes.

e. Ask people to remain in teams, to read the following passages from John, and to answer the questions below, remembering what they have read in chapter 6:

· 10:11. What do you learn from this verse about the meaning of Jesus' command in John 21:15, "Feed my lambs"?

· 13:36-38. How far does Peter promise to go as a follower of Jesus? What is Jesus calling Peter to do in 21:19 when he commands "Follow me"?

· 15:13. How does Jesus define love in 15:13? Could that be what Jesus means by love in 21:15-17? If so, why does he ask Peter whether he loves Jesus?

· 18:15-18, 25-27. The setting of Jesus' conversation with Peter in 21:15-19 is the charcoal fire on which Jesus cooked breakfast in 21:9. What prior event involving Peter took place around a charcoal fire?

Have each team share with the entire group one important thing they learned from studying these passages.

3. *Enlivening the Story and Reflecting.* Ask the teams to experiment with different ways of saying the words of Jesus and Peter in John 21:15-17. What feelings do they think are most appropriate to their words in light of activity e above? What stories can they tell each other of experiencing similar feelings towards another person?

4. *Creative Response.* Ask the teams to each develop a responsive reading in which one voice tells the story and another interrupts the telling at appropriate points with the passages listed in activity e.

5. *Ministering Through Biblical Storytelling.* On Video Segment VI people tell some of the stories in this course in various settings. After viewing the video segment ask the members of your group: "What opportunities have you found over the past weeks to pass the story on? Which stories did you tell and in which settings?" Also inquire: "Did you find opportunities other than those illustrated in the video? Can you think of still others?"

6. *Suggestions for Going Further.* Use the model established for the preceding sessions. Since there are no more sessions in the course, ask participants to agree with one other participant on a time to meet next week in order to share the story and their personal connecting experiences.

7. *Closing.* Ask a team to volunteer to share their responsive reading. Invite a team with a very different responsive reading to share theirs.

What Wondrous Love Is This?

Text: Rev. Alexander Means, 1835   Melody from "Southern Harmony," 1835

1 What won - drous love is this, O my soul, O my soul?
2 To God and to the Lamb I will sing, I will sing;
3 And when from death I'm free, I'll sing on, I'll sing on;

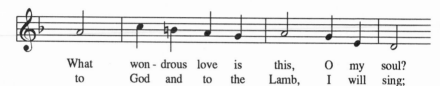

What won - drous love is this, O my soul?
to God and to the Lamb, I will sing;
and when from death I'm free, I'll sing on;

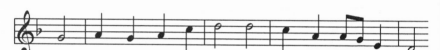

What won - drous love is this that caused the Lord of bliss
to God and to the Lamb who is the great I AM,
and when from death I'm free, I'll sing and joy - ful be,

to bear the dread - ful curse for my soul, for my soul;
while mil - lions join the theme, I will sing, I will sing;
and through e - ter - ni - ty I'll sing on, I'll sing on!

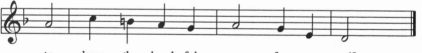

to bear the dread - ful curse for my soul?
while mil - lions join the theme, I will sing.
And through e - ter - ni - ty, I'll sing on.